O&

ASTROLOGY'S
Complete Book of
SELF-DEFENCE

Robert Parry is an instructor in the health
and relaxation aspects of Tai Chi, and a
practising astrologer, achieving diploma
qualifications from the Faculty of
Astrological Studies. His main concern is the
promotion of astrology to a general
readership — hence the emphasis in his
work on defence and debate. He has
developed a witty well-informed
thought-provoking and accessible style. He
is a member of the Astrological Association
of Great Britain and lives in Kent.

Cover illustration by Warron Prentice
Cartoons by Robert Parry

ASTROLOGY'S
Complete Book of
SELF-DEFENCE

Robert Parry

quantum

LONDON • NEW YORK • TORONTO • SYDNEY

quantum

An imprint of W. Foulsham & Co. Ltd.,
Yeovil Road, Slough, Berkshire SL1 4JH

ISBN 0–572–01586–0
Copyright © 1990 Robert Parry

Printed in Great Britain at St Edmundsbury Press, Bury St Edmunds

To the ancestors for their wisdom and perseverance, and the two women in my life for their patience and understanding

CONTENTS

Part Two SELF-DEFENCE

Part Three WHERE IS ASTROLOGY GOING?

ACKNOWLEDGEMENT

The author and publisher wish to thank the Faculty of Astrological Studies for permission to reproduce its Code of Ethics on page 50.

INTRODUCTION

This book is intended for anyone with an interest in what I believe to be one of the greatest, most enduring and most exciting ideas known to mankind. It is for anyone with just the tiniest glimmer of faith in a meaningful universe in which he or she has a part to play, no matter how small, no matter how humble. It is for anyone who doesn't believe that life is simply the outcome of blind and brutal forces of chaos and chance. These are so often given in our times as an excuse for dullness or resignation, or for a stifling cynicism that crushes all personal creativity and joy.

If you believe you 'belong' in the universe; if you believe in the dignity of the human spirit, then you are an astrologer. Welcome. This book will help you to defend yourself, and make your position clear.

We are all astrologers. Whether we like it or not, or whether we know it or not, we have the experience of the sky, the earth beneath it and the cycles of the days, months and seasons deeply programmed into our psyches, part of our mental software since time began. It is this experience of the natural world, its rhythms and changes, which shaped the most ancient philosophies, and which still shapes the most modern patterns of human behaviour, feelings and desires. Shut off from the natural world, we can become sick, disoriented and lost. The rapport of humankind with the environment is the human experience of the skies, and this experience of the skies is the individual's claim to the title astrologer, as I shall be using the term in this book. For if indeed we are all travellers on the spaceship earth — as we are so often reminded — then we all need to be navigators of a sort, too.

Many experts in self-defence would probably agree with me that the ancient Chinese system of Tai Chi Chuan is still the supreme form of martial art. Those trained to the peak of excellence in karate, judo or boxing, can pose no threat whatsoever to the fully developed Tai Chi master, who will appear to block and deflect every effort of an opponent with the utmost ease. Trying to overpower such a person is like trying to catch a shadow or grasp the wind. Indeed, to see Tai Chi being practised or taught is rather like observing a wholly natural process: a graceful slow-motion 'dance', featuring remarkably soft and delicate movements, called in Tai Chi a 'form'. But then in combat, these slow and delicate movements can suddenly become swift devastating blocks or parries followed up if necessary by counter moves of great force and energy. These are generated from the centre of the body via a unique combination of vitality, concentration and most important, inner calm.

The key to perfect self-defence therefore, according to Tai Chi philosophy, is a combination of knowledge, relaxation and self-control. Through knowledge and relaxation comes anticipation, and through anticipation comes correct and perfect reaction.

Enthusiasts of astrology often find themselves confronted by others who are hostile to their cause, and the ability to defend oneself in such a situation comes only through clarity, and perhaps a similar degree of self-confidence and relaxation as found in the art of Tai Chi. Many, if not all of the qualities so vital to the warrior on the field of battle are also essential to the enthusiast in debate, or to the professional at his or her desk. Without such qualities you cannot hope to sustain any kind of position in the face of adversity. The cultivation of such preparedness, along with the necessary arguments of defence that sustain it, are what you will find in these pages.

Real astrology, as distinct from show-biz and journalistic horoscopes which most people wrongly associate with the subject, still remains rather a remote activity in our times. And the feverish search for 'proof' and scientific respectability that is currently in vogue among professionals in the field is not really of much help to the public either, being comprehensible only to a handful of statisticians and specialists. Sometimes, too, professional astrologers will feel no need to defend themselves at all, or give reasons, if compelled, for an interest in such a strange and, to many, utterly daft occupation. The astrologer might feel able to bluff a way out or simply refuse, rather pompously, to discuss the matter on anything less than a purely scientific level. This does neither the astrologer nor astrology much credit, however, since, to an opponent who is a confirmed cynic, such a posture looks highly suspect.

'Give you a reason on compulsion! If reasons were as plenty as blackberries I would give no man a reason upon compulsion.' So states the lovable but totally appalling Sir John Falstaff in Shakespeare's play. And every one of us when pressed and void of convincing arguments can slip into this mould.

As an astrologer, I have always thought it a good idea to be able to explain and argue for astrology on a conversational level, in a way which is easily understood. This means debate, lively discussion, a little humour as well. And if it is apparent that the general public needs to learn more about 'real' astrology from time to time, then it seems equally apparent that astrologers must teach and communicate in a language both modern and comprehensible.

Yes, this book is intended to inform and, if possible, to educate; but above all else it is to be enjoyed. Inordinate seriousness and gravity are not the ways to relaxation or self-control. Nor should the discussion of great ideas, even ideas of the most profound kind, such as those expressed within the compass of astrology, ever be incompatible with simple good cheer and happiness.

PART ONE
WHAT IS ASTROLOGY?

CHAPTER 1
THE EXPERIENCE OF ASTROLOGY

*Very slowly the sky darkens, leaving a purple glow along the
silhouetted eastern horizon. One by one, tiny jewels of light
appear, the brightest and greatest first, until very soon the entire
sky is filled with stars. Perhaps a bright planet or two will be
shining out, or the great pearl of the moon vying with the
mysterious glow of our own galactic wheel, the Milky Way.
Why do we so often pause and look up and around the sky before
hurrying indoors on such a night? Why at such times do lovers
positively ooze tenderness, or children gaze from bedroom
windows long past bed time? Why does old Blue Eyes ask you to
fly him to the moon and swing upon a star, or an entire global
souvenir industry suddenly spring up overnight at the return of
Halley's comet? Why do thousands of amateur-guided telescopes
turn skywards each evening from every part of the globe, or
inebriated travellers at sea, far from home, suddenly look up and
wax poetical at the sight of the night sky?*

'The stars! Oh, by the Lord, look at the stars!' a voice suddenly
said, with a heavy sing-song accent. It belonged to a young man
who had been Tonio Kröger's neighbour at dinner in the salon.
His dress was very simple, his eyes were red, and he had the
moist and chilly look of a person who had just bathed. With
nervous and self-conscious movements he had taken unto
himself an astonishing quantity of lobster omelette. Now he
leaned on the rail beside Tonio Kröger and looked up at the
skies, holding his chin between thumb and forefinger. Beyond a
doubt he was in one of the rare and festal and edifying moods
that cause the barriers between man and man to fall: when the
heart opens even to the stranger, and the mouth utters that
which otherwise it would blush to speak . . .

17

'Look, my dear sir, just look at the stars! There they stahd and glitter. My goodness, the whole sky is full of theb! And I ask you, when you stahd and look up at theb, and realize that bany of theb are a hundred tibes larger thad the earth, how does it bake you feel? Yes, we have invented the telegraph and the telephone and all the triumphs of our bodern times. But when we look up there we have to recogdize and understahd that we are worbs, biserable worbs and dothing else. Am I right, sir or ab I wrong? Yes, we are worbs,' he answered himself, and nodded meekly and abjectly in the direction of the firmament.

(From *Tonio Kröger*, by Thoman Mann)

Often it takes exceptional circumstances to open our eyes afresh to the miracle of the skies. Reactions range from awe and tranquillity, to a sense of insignificance and inferiority, depending on one's mood at the time. Some of us adore the night sky, others fear and dread it. Some people feel the need to immerse themselves in its vastness, others are aware of an equally persuasive urge to ignore or to rationalise its mystery through the language of science. Often the pull of the skies is an unconscious one. Some people sleepwalk over rooftops, following the moon, others find its presence almost magnetic, irresistibly engaging without quite knowing how or why — and not only 'lunatics' but, if we care to admit it, most of us at times of emotional intensity and excitement.

As the dance surged heavily on, Ursula was aware of some influence looking in upon her. Something was looking at her. Some powerful, glowing sight was looking right into her, not upon her, but right at her. Out of the great distance, and yet imminent, the powerful, overwhelming watch was kept upon her. And she danced on with Skrebensky, while the great white watching continued, balancing all in its revelation.

'The moon has risen,' said Anton, as the music ceased, and they found themselves suddenly stranded, like bits of jetsam on a shore. She turned, and saw a great white moon looking at her over the hill. And her breast opened to it, she was cleaved like a transparent jewel to its light. She stood filled with the full moon, offering herself. Her two breasts opened to make way for it, her body opened wide like a quivering anemone, a soft, dilated invitation touched by the moon. She wanted the moon to fill in to her, she wanted more, more communion with the moon, consummation. But Skrebensky put his arm round her

18

and led her away. He put a big dark cloak round her, and sat holding her hand, whilst the moonlight streamed above the glowing fires.

(From *The Rainbow*, by D.H. Lawrence)

The moon, of course, is continually popular with poets — often to the point of infatuation. That most visible of concepts in astrological lore, the moon has always been associated with reflection, with receiving and retaining images and feelings — and thus its age-old correspondence with the metal silver, used in mirrors and, more recently, photographic film. The old Romantic poets especially would perceive a reflection of their own restless spirits in the changing, wayward phases of the moon.

Art thou pale for weariness
Of climbing heaven and gazing on the earth,
Wandering companionless
Among the stars that have a different birth, —
And ever changing, like a joyless eye
That finds no object worth its constancy? (Shelley)

The poets speak our minds, the way we all instinctively feel at moments but cannot always put into rational terms. Of course we can choose to run from the irrational, as many do when the flame of passion and intensity seems too threatening. But we loose a part of ourselves when we do so, and we become poorer as a consequence, shut in behind the walls of 'realism' and sobriety that we build as a defence, primarily against pain, but consequently against joy and inspiration as well.

Our experience of the skies, the astrological experience in its most fundamental form, is our love affair with life, with the pleasure and the pain. For if we can love our friends, our family, those closest to us who are, after all, just so much flesh and bones according to purely biological analysis, then is it really so strange to love our planet and the family to which it likewise belongs? To our earth and the family of the

19

skies we owe our very existence. Should we be averse to loving such entities, no matter how remote? Certainly, our present age, in its urgency for a new and popular ecological consciousness, needs to rekindle that particular old flame. Surely even the most cynical among us, if he loves nothing else, loves himself — yet this too is a love affair with the skies . . .

> The body of a man is his house; the architect who builds it is the astral world. The carpenters are at one time Jupiter, at another Venus; at one time Taurus, at another Orion. Man is a Sun and a Moon and a heaven filled with stars; the world is a man, and the light of the Sun and the stars is his body. (Paracelsus)

We love the skies even as we love ourselves. The connection has always been felt. The very phenomenon of mankind has grown out of such blissful infatuation. The builders of the great megalithic stone circles in Europe were totally love-struck with the earth and the skies and their place within it.

The moon, the sun, and of course the wandering planets have all figured as sources of fascination and veneration at various times throughout history — and long before history, when people began to notice relationships between certain celestial occurrences and the moods and changes within themselves and the community. Men and women and their gods grew alongside one another as a result. As humans came to know the skies, so too did they come to recognise the various parts within. The gods came to personify these parts, the sun, the moon, Jupiter, Saturn, Mercury, Mars and Venus — each a reflection of a desire, a wish, a thought.

We see this closeness, this intimacy between the person and the natural forces of the psyche, the gods, throughout history — and as recently as the Renaissance period. In the wonderful paintings and sculpture of those times, the skies and their inhabitants would often appear in frescoes and on ceilings. The gods looked down from a starry vault, a blue and golden hemisphere high above the profane world. The human vision was naturally skyward, the individual's spirit naturally elevated towards the stars. The beings that represented our longings and desires, our fears and our sorrows, our inspiration and our sustenance, all dwelled above us. Our entire spiritual and cultural inheritance is from the heavens. So many of the words in our language come from them: martial (Mars), jovial (Jupiter), mercurial (Mercury), venal (Venus), saturnine and Saturday (Saturn), Monday and lunatic (Moon/*Luna*) to name but a few. Even our greatest religious festival in the West coincides with the 'rebirth' of the sun each year, when it starts to visibly increase in height above the horizon — Christmas Eve.

As naturally as a man loved his wife, his children, his parents, their individual characters and the community to which they belonged, so too did he love his planet, the sun, the moon, and the great family of the skies that seemed to fill his spirit with such variety and diversification.

The veneration still continues, make no mistake about that. Only today, apart from those quick, surreptitious glances at the horoscopes in newspapers, most of us have slightly more furtive means towards exercising our affections. For some it is 'the great outdoors', camping, rambling, fishing by night; for some it is the 'occult', magical ceremony, bare botties dancing in the moonlight. For others it is a search for an all-embracing oblivion in alcohol or drugs; or actual lunacy — ask anyone who has worked in a mental asylum how the night passes when there's a full moon.

Then, for some, it is building a small telescope and sitting with hot-water bottle and thermos flask through long nights of patient observation: the amateur astronomers, bless us all! And let's not forget the UFO enthusiasts and the enormous publishing industry that has grown up to satisfy their needs. Even though most sightings have perfectly banal explanations, almost everyone has a UFO story to relate, with some even claiming to have been whisked away and made love to by amorous extraterrestrials. Devotion indeed!

21

Then, more seriously, remember that the national flags of so many nations, under which so many people have fought and died, will contain a star more often than not, while the remainder tend to draw upon the solar circle, the lunar crescent or that other and most potent of astrological symbols, the cross, for their basic design.

Next time you watch commercial TV, just try counting the number of times stars, suns or moons, of one sort or another appear in advertisements. Those in the advertising industry have long known the subliminal appeal of astronomical symbolism. People are attracted by the skies; they are comforted, or disturbed, or enchanted — but they rarely ignore a burst of starlight on their TV screens, or a swift blessing from heaven. The very celebrities that appear on our screens, those heroes and even god-like figures we worship so avidly are called 'stars'. Astrology sells.

But the astrological experience is also a direct one, we all feel it. At times we feel it a lot. Luck is a reality. I know a man who went right through the card at a race meeting one afternoon, then came up with one or two winning greyhounds the same evening; went to celebrate at his local club afterwards, promptly won the jackpot on a fruit machine, and finally, while picking up some late take-aways for his children, found a banknote on the pavement outside the shop!

Yes, that was what is called a lucky day. But the boot can be on the other foot. And when things do go badly, how they go! We all know the feeling: times when nothing works for us. Misfortune and sheer bad luck seem to dog us incessantly, with no rational explanation whatsoever. Who can deny such periods! As the Bard says . . .

> When sorrows come,
> They come not single spies,
> But in battalions. (*Hamlet*)

Certainly we feel we have worked out the laws of chance

quite well, the way the dice must fall; but real-life experience, uncooperative as ever, does not as yet seem to concur. The fact of the matter is that once you start to look a little closely at real life, and real astrology as it seeks to interpret it, the laws of chance go straight out the window. In their place, many highly interesting questions start to arise, questions which really won't go away, unless you choose to ignore the evidence there before your eyes.

Why, for example, are astrologers able to successfully interpret the character of an individual by analysing the positions of the planets at the moment of birth? Why are they able to forecast those periods of outstandingly good or absolutely abysmal 'luck'? How is it that certain astrological principles are vindicated constantly in experimentation and statistical research? Why, and how, are certain specialist astrologers able to locate lost articles, or missing animals, or answer questions on the viability of relationships, contracts, business ventures or real estate? How are they able to do this time and time again as a matter of routine, and — what's more — earn a respectable living doing so for private clients day after day, the world over? Why, in brief, does astrology work?

These are questions worthy of the best of inquiring minds in any age, our own notwithstanding; the person who refuses to ask them would be better off working at the zoo teaching ostriches to bury their heads in the sand.

Ask the questions, however, and you are already on the journey of independence and self-discovery; you have started to comprehend your place in the scheme of things, willing to admit you can control your destiny by understanding and moving intelligently within the laws of nature, not battling against them like some monstrous spoilt child who demands the whole universe to revolve around his own selfish, egocentric existence. Ask those questions, and you have already begun to rediscover the experience, the incredible, fascinating and hugely rewarding experience of astrology.

CHAPTER 2

TOOLS OF THE TRADE

Before going any further, let us just take a brief look at the nuts and bolts of real astrology as it has been practised throughout the centuries and, indeed, as it is largely still practised today.

There are various branches of astrology in existence today. Discounting, as we must do, the largely worthless horoscopes found in newspapers and magazines, the most widespread variety is called Natal astrology. This deals with the character of individual people and often attempts, with varying degrees of success, to predict the future trends in their lives. The branch of astrology that deals with nations and large groups of people is called Mundane astrology, while that which deals with separate questions concerning journeys, lost articles, etc., and attempts to provide definite and clear-cut answers to these, is called Horary astrology. The branch called Electional astrology deals with the timing of future events, such as the starting of a business, the laying of a foundation stone, etc. And Financial astrology deals, just as the name suggests, with trends in economics, stock market and commodity prices.

The basis of all astrological work is the Birth Chart. This is an accurate map of the sky for the exact date, time and place of birth. Now this can be the birth of a person like you or me, or it could also be the birth of a nation, or of a limited company, or even of an idea or a question. The central principle of astrology is that the start of anything, that very special moment when something new comes into existence, is absolutely paramount in significance.

The moment of birth is like a seed, containing everything that is to come and grow from that seed. The astrologer's work, therefore, is not unlike that of a botanist or an expert in horticulture. Careful examination can tell him quite a lot. A botanist will tell you the species by examining the seed; an astrologer will tell you the personality by examining the birth chart. The botanist will explain the kind of conditions in which the seed will flourish; the astrologer will speculate on what kind of work and environment will suit his or her client. The botanist will tell you how the seed will grow, and what the mature plant or tree will look like; the astrologer will tell you the way events are most likely to unfold into the future — forecasting.

A DAY AT THE OFFICE

So just how is an astrologer's chart put together? What sort of information does it contain? Figure 1 shows the construction of a typical birth chart, stage by stage. We begin by freezing the moment in time at which our birth takes place. This is the situation in Figure 1a, basically a picture of the sky as it was at the time in relation to the earth beneath it. Against the known background of fixed stars, you have the sun, in this case just setting in the west; the moon high up in the southern sky; and finally some of the planets, of which there are nine in all including the earth. The planets are our nearest neighbours in space, members of our solar system which shine by the reflected light of the sun. Many of them are easily visible to the naked eye if you know where and when to look. They will appear to change position from night to night while the stars, which are distant suns, will retain the same formations. The word 'planet' means 'wanderer'.

In Figure 1b you have the narrow band of stars called the zodiac marked in, divided up into its well-known and celebrated 'signs', twelve equal sections, within which all the

25

Figure 1a.   Freezing a moment in time

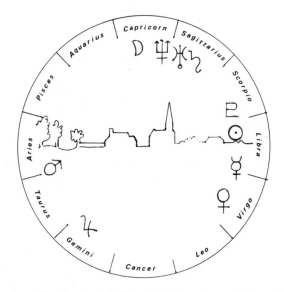

*Figure 1b.   The 'frozen moment' with the signs of the zodiac and
the planets shown*

important bodies, sun, moon and planets are invariably
situated. Of course, some of the signs and planets would
have been out of sight and beneath the horizon at the
moment of birth, but these are still considered important
and have now been included in our picture to complete the
circle of the heavens. The planets themselves are now shown

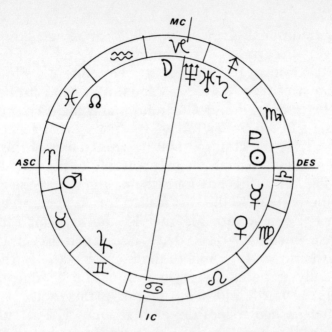

Figure 1c.   The horizontal and vertical axes of the chart have been drawn in

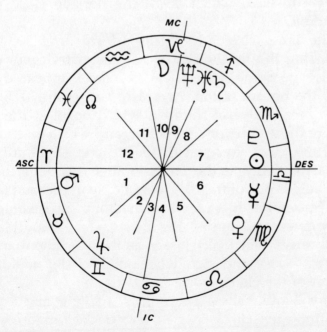

Figure 1d.   The final chart includes the twelve astrological houses

in their traditional glyph form, the symbols recognised by astrologers the world over: Mercury ☿ ; Venus ♀ ; Mars ♂ ; Jupiter ♃ ; Saturn ♄ ; Uranus ♅ ; Neptune ♆ ; Pluto ♇ . Therefore we have Mercury, Venus, Mars and Jupiter beneath the horizon in our illustration, and the other bodies, including sun and moon, above it.

In Figure 1c the all important horizontal axis of the chart has been drawn. Roughly corresponding to the actual horizon in Figure 1a, this line joins the points where the zodiac meets the horizon in the east (called the Ascendant) and in the west (Descendant). Meanwhile, the local meridian — that great imaginary circle that passes overhead and joins the north and south points of the horizon — helps to form the equally important verticle axis of the chart, passing through the north and south points of the zodiac as seen from that particular location at that time. This is marked MC/IC on the chart. Any planets found close to these lines are considered especially strong like the moon in this case, and the sun also, which is on the horizon close to the Descendant.

By the time we get to Figure 1d we have something approaching the finished chart as most astrologers would recognise it. Some added features have appeared here, namely the houses of the chart. The houses are sections of space, again twelve in number, which begin at the rising degree of the zodiac, or Ascendant, and which extend right around the 'clock' to cover the entire sky. There are many systems for dividing the chart in this way, but the one shown here is one of the most commonly used, the Placidus House System, as it is called, named after its seventeenth-century inventor. Houses, like the signs, are important and the astrologer will look closely at the placement of each planet by house and sign when judging the quality and character of the chart.

Figures 2 and 3 show two typical working charts as you would find them on the astrologer's desk. You know what to look out for by now. Firstly there are the planets (for

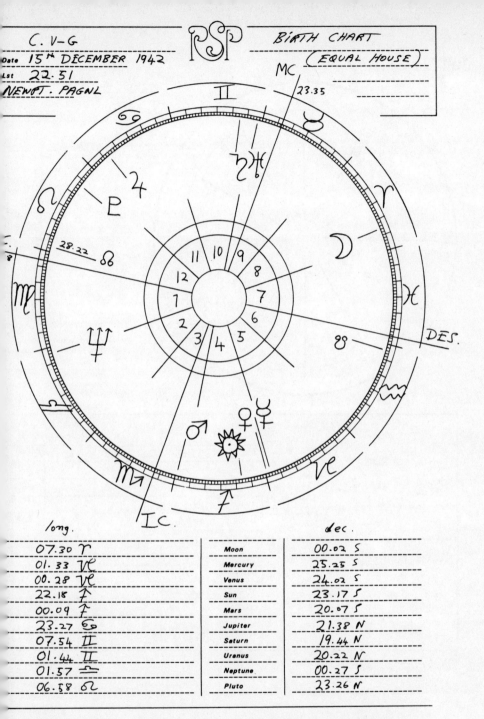

Figure 2. Typical example of a birth chart as an astrologer would draw it.
The coordinates of the planets and signs of the zodiac are listed in the table

BIRTH CHART

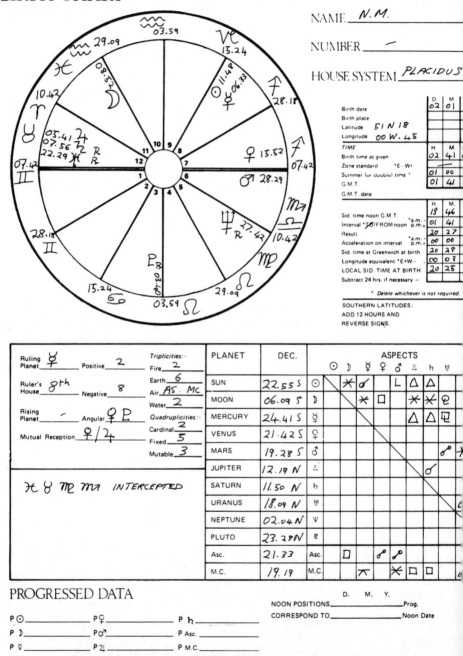

NAME _N. M._

NUMBER _____

HOUSE SYSTEM _PLACIDUS_

	D.	M.
Birth date	02	01
Birth place		
Latitude	51 N 18	
Longitude	00 W. 45	

TIME	H.	M.	
Birth time as given	02	41	
Zone standard *E – W+			
Summer (or double) time *	01	00	
G.M.T.	01	41	

G.M.T. date	H.	M.
Sid. time noon G.M.T.	18	46
Interval *TO/FROM noon *a.m. p.m.+	01	41
Result	20	27
Acceleration on interval *a.m. p.m.+	00	00
Sid. time at Greenwich at birth	20	28
Longitude equivalent *E+W--	00	03
LOCAL SID. TIME AT BIRTH	20	25
Subtract 24 hrs. if necessary −		

* Delete whichever is not required.

SOUTHERN LATITUDES:
ADD 12 HOURS AND
REVERSE SIGNS.

Ruling Planet ☿ Positive 2
Ruler's House 8th Negative 8
Rising Planet ___ Angular ♀ ♇
Mutual Reception ♀ / ♃

Triplicities: ·
Fire 2
Earth 6
Air AS. MC
Water 2
Quadruplicities: ·
Cardinal 2
Fixed 5
Mutable 3

♓ ♉ ♏ ♐ INTERCEPTED

PLANET	DEC.	ASPECTS							
		☉	☽	☿	♀	♂	♃	♄	♅
SUN	22.55 S	☉	✱	☌			L	△	△
MOON	06.09 S	☽			✱	□		✱	✱ ☍
MERCURY	24.41 S	☿						△	△ 🜍
VENUS	21.42 S	♀							
MARS	19.28 S	♂							☍
JUPITER	12.19 N	♃						☌	
SATURN	11.50 N	♄							
URANUS	18.09 N	♅							
NEPTUNE	02.04 N	♆							
PLUTO	23.28 N	♇							
Asc.	21.33	Asc.	□		☌	☍			
M.C.	19.19	M.C.		⊼		✱	□	□	

PROGRESSED DATA

P ☉ _____   P ♀ _____   P ♄ _____

P ☽ _____   P ♂ _____   P Asc. _____

P ☿ _____   P ♃ _____   P M.C. _____

D.   M.   Y.
NOON POSITIONS _____ Prog.
CORRESPOND TO _____ Noon Date

Figure 3. A further example of a typical birth chart. The coordinates of the planets and signs of the zodiac are shown inside the chart wheel itself

convenience, the sun and moon are called planets in astrology) with their exact positions marked in degrees and minutes. These coordinates can be listed separately, as in Figure 2, or they can appear inside the chart wheel itself, as in Figure 3. Always there is the circle of the zodiac, shown on the outer rim, the twelve signs from Aries through to Pisces. And finally there is the system of houses, the divisions within the wheel, like twelve spokes radiating from the centre.

The sky is always changing, of course, as the earth rotates beneath it, once on its axis every twenty-four hours, so that all these positions can vary, not only from hour to hour but from minute to minute, giving rise to any number of possible birth charts. For example, if you refer back to Figure 1 for a moment, and imagine the chart, say, ten minutes onwards in time, Mars would then be rising, placed no longer in the 1st house but in the 12th, while the sun would have set beneath the horizon, no longer in the 7th house but now in the 6th. This is why we each have a distinct and unique astrological make-up, each born at our own particular time and place.

The planets themselves are also in constant motion against the background of the zodiac. Their individual speeds vary greatly. The moon, for example, makes one complete circuit of the zodiac in around twenty-eight days, while the 'wise old man' of the zodiac, Saturn, takes as long as thirty years. Also, each planet has a distinct and definite character which is modified by the sign and house in which it is placed. Mars, for example, is the planet of aggression, extraversion, self-confidence and sexuality. It has numerous associations — for example with the sign Aries; the metal iron; with fire, the colour red and with the ruby, and many, many more. The same goes for all the other planets. The following table on page 32 is a list of just a few of these features, 'correlations' as they are called.

Angular relationships between planets are also very important. These relationships are called 'aspects' in astrologi-

PLANET	QUALITIES	COLOURS	METAL	STONES
MOON	Imagination, Fantasy Reflection, Thought	White Sea tones	Silver	Moonstone Pearl
MERCURY	Communication, Business Agility, Craft	Variegated Yellow	Quicksilver	Onyx Beryl
VENUS	Comfort, Love, Desire Beauty, Proportion	Blue Green	Copper	Sapphire Aquamarine
SUN	Splendour, Creativity Pride, Diplomacy	Yellow Red	Gold	Topaz Garnet
MARS	Force, Aggression Courage, Sexuality	Red	Iron	Ruby Diamond
JUPITER	Joy, Expansion, Law, Study Preservation, Philosophy	Green Purple	Tin	Emerald Marble
SATURN	Age, Tradition, Slowness Death, Neurosis, Limits	Black	Lead	Lapis Quartz
URANUS	Change, Revolution Originality, Invention	Metallic		
NEPTUNE	Mystery, the Unconscious Illusion, Inspiration	Camouflage		
PLUTO	Power, Hidden Forces Implacability, Destiny	Hidden		

cal jargon. An aspect blends the characteristics of bodies in certain ways. For example, a Square (90-degree) aspect between two planets indicates tension or disagreement between them, whereas a Trine (120-degree) aspect indicates sympathy and cooperation (see Figure 4). There are about a dozen different types of aspect, each corresponding to a precise division of the circle. Figure 3 has the aspects for that particular chart listed in the square grid to the lower right of the chart wheel.

As we have seen, the zodiac itself contains twelve signs: Aries, Taurus, and so on. An important point is that these signs are distinct from the old star groups which are still referred to in astronomical maps and text books. These star groups, or constellations as they are called, can bear the same names as the popular signs of the zodiac but they are based on different coordinates. The astrologer's zodiac actually moves with time, albeit slowly, against the background of fixed stars, ensuring, no matter what minor variations

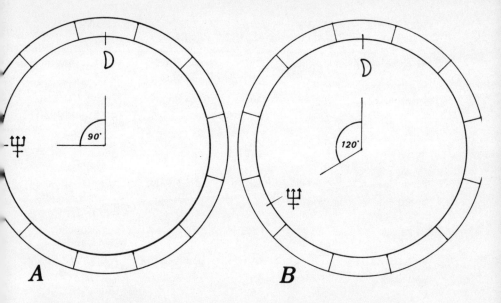

Figure 4. a) Example of a 90-degree angle between two planets, or
'square aspect' b) Example of a 120-degree angle between two planets,
or 'trine aspect'

occur between the relation of the earth to the sun, that the zodiac always stays in touch with the passage of the seasons: spring, summer, autumn and winter.

The twelve signs themselves have many sub-divisions. First there is that seasonal division into what are called Cardinal, Fixed, and Mutable signs; then there are six positive and six negative signs; and also there is the division into elements: Fire, Earth, Air and Water. All these features help to determine the unique character of each sign, which will in turn modify the character of any planet located within the boundaries of that sign.

There are many other divisions of the signs that need not concern us here. Suffice it to say there is an awful lot that the astrologer has to keep in mind, and long ago it was found that the easiest way to remember all the possible permutations was to employ a simple mnemonic device for each sign, usually an animal or creature of some kind.

TWELVE SECTIONS	SEASONAL QUALITY	ELEMENT	POLARITY	MNEMONIC DEVICE
The 1st Section	is Cardinal,	FIRE	and Positive	A RAM (Aries)
The 2nd Section	is Fixed,	EARTH	and Negative	A BULL (Taurus)
The 3rd Section	is Mutable,	AIR	and Positive	TWINS (Gemini)
The 4th Section	is Cardinal,	WATER	and Negative	A CRAB (Cancer)
The 5th Section	is Fixed,	FIRE	and Positive	A LION (Leo)
The 6th Section	is Mutable,	EARTH	and Negative	A YOUNG WOMAN (Virgo)
The 7th Section	is Cardinal,	AIR	and Positive	SCALES (Libra)
The 8th Section	is Fixed,	WATER	and Negative	A SCORPION (Scorpio)
The 9th Section	is Mutable,	FIRE	and Positive	AN ARCHER (Sagittarius)
The 10th Section	is Cardinal,	EARTH	and Negative	A GOAT (Capricorn)
The 11th Section	is Fixed,	AIR	and Positive	WATER POURER (Aquarius)
The 12th Section	is Mutable,	WATER	and Negative	FISHES (Pisces)

And what about the houses? Well, each of these actually relates to a particular field of human activity. For example, an astrologer looks to the house placement of each planet to locate the area of life in which it will most likely manifest, whether in career (10th house), or in partnerships (7th house), or with family (4th house), and so on. Every human activity, every facet of being alive has its place under one of the twelve houses. The origins of these correspondences are historical in nature, but like the zodiac they are actually based on the old associations with the four quarters of heaven and the four seasons. Despite many assertions to the contrary, they do follow a strictly logical pattern. The table on page 35 shows some of the main correlations for each house.

The distinct and diverse astrological nature of every human being on this earth is a result of all these factors combining: planets, houses and signs. A useful metaphor is to think of a stage production. The planets are the actors; the houses make up the scenery; and the zodiac is the theatre in which it all takes place. The permutations, the possibilities are endless.

HOUSE NUMBER	LOCATION IN THE CHART (NORTHERN HEMISPHERE)		FIELD OF ACTIVITY
1st	East	Place of sunrise	Self, Appearance, Image, Beginnings
2nd			Material affairs, Finance, Resources
3rd			Communications, Brethren, Study
4th	North	Midnight	Inner experience, Home, Parents
5th			Creativity, Children, Speculation
6th			Service, Care, Health
7th	West	Place of sunset	Partners, Rivals, the 'Other Self'
8th			Resources of others, Death
9th			Expansion, Travel, Wisdom
10th	South	Sun at noon	External Sphere, Reputation, Career
11th			Ambitions, Friendships
12th			Secrets, Restrictions, Guilt

Later on, we are going to look at the way astrologers make use of this kind of information, firstly to judge character and personality from the chart, and secondly to speculate on future trends by expanding the chart in certain ways. But as you can see already, it is absolutely essential, imperative, for the astrologer to have access to precise birth data, including the exact time and place as well as date. This is why horoscopes in magazines and papers are really of little value, if any at all, using only the sun signs of its readers, in other words the month of birth only, regardless of even the year of birth, as a basis for so-called predictions. Individual charting is impossible under such conditions.

No . . . genuine astrology is *not* to be found in the Sunday supplements or, sadly, even on television, all relatively recent developments in the worlds of journalism and show biz. Genuine astrology — and you've already taken a glimpse of it here — has in fact a long and distinguished history, with an even more exciting present. And this is what we are going to take a look at next: all part of our determined bid to answer that most intriguing of questions, 'What is Astrology?'

CHAPTER 3
FROM MAGIC TO MOCKERY

Picture the scene. It is sunrise on a chilly day in late winter. It seems as if the entire community, anyone who is anybody, is gathered here on the vast plains about the circle of stones. The elders and wise women have been ever-vigilant, as they always are and always have been. This morning they will know exactly where the sun will rise, exactly how the great moon will appear. The calendar and the oracle speak through the stones to them; the heavens dictate the time for planting the seed, and the new year's crops will be sown. The ceremony proceeds: the sacrifice, the music, the chanting. The earth beneath seems to resonate with the importance and the magic of this moment. Later there will be dancing and festivities, and priests will attend to the observatory, adjusting wooden marker stakes, taking measurements, discussing the latest developments and progressive changes that they and their ancestors have noted in the skies over millennia of seasons coming and going.

Thousands of years ago, before we have any real records of history to go by, this might well have been the picture in so many parts of Europe on such important occasions throughout the year. Other places on the globe would have enjoyed their own particular local observances: whole communities clustered around temples, pyramids, sacred groves, churches; always oriented to the cardinal points, always aligned with the sun and the great turning wheel of the sky. The world was one of magic and ecstasy, love for nature and the determination to understand and work within its inscrutable framework of time and change. Here is the origin of the astrological experience: surely as much in veneration and love as in fear and superstition.

I for one have always felt dissatisfied with the usual explanation historians give for the existence in the past of pursuits such as magic, religion or astrology. We are urged to believe that the main driving force behind ancient pre-historic communities and their sky-oriented cultures was fear. Fear ruled everything. The gods of nature were wor-shipped and propitiated through fear. Temples and great stone circles were erected through fear. Fear gave rise to every personification of every natural force, from lightning to the seasons themselves. What nonsense!

Although insecurity was certainly felt by ancient peoples at times of war or natural disaster, the fear-principle is grossly over-stated in our view of antiquity. Perhaps this is owing to our present attitude to life, and the dreadful and unprecedented uncertainties that characterise our culture and times. It is an attitude and an approach to history that is forgivable, but it tells us little of those who have gone before.

Conventional scholarship leans towards the view that astrology began in the old Mesopotamian civilisations of the Middle-East sometime around the second millennium BC. But this is by no means universally accepted among his-torians, nor among astrologers themselves. All we really know is that astrology emerged here around this time as a system that had already reached a high standard of com-plexity, hinting, therefore, at a much older origin. In fact, it may already have peaked and have fallen into a degenerate and decadant phase by the time it seeped into popular usage in the superstitious worlds of the late Egyptian and Babylonian civilisations.

Our involvement with the skies is as old as the human species. There is evidence of the phases of the moon being recorded via notches on bone as early as 15 000 BC. Much later, there is evidence of a preoccupation with astrology in the ancient Vedic and Taoist literature of India and China, and, as we have seen, in the megalithic stones of north-west Europe, which have now been shown beyond any shadow of doubt to have been highly sophisticated observatories as well as religious sites. All these have as great, if not a greater claim to antiquity than Babylonian astrology. The stone circles of Avebury and Stonehenge in England, for example, are currently thought to date from around 4000–2000 BC.

However, it is from the Mesopotamian and the later classical cultures that most of our modern astrological system is derived. The spread of astrology to the Greek and Roman worlds occurred in the centuries immediately prior to the Christian era. And here it was that the birth chart as we know it began to take shape, so that by the time of Manilius and Ptolemy, that is by the first and second centuries AD, the astrologer's work is quite recognisable and familiar to those in practice today.

In those times, astrology as a subject went hand in hand with many other disciplines which we would nowadays consider unconnected. Medicine, for example, was deeply entwined with astrological lore. The great second-century physician, Galen, used his doctrine of the four humours extensively. These were the four elements of astrology, and influenced medical thought for centuries. Chinese medicine is still based on an observation of the elements and how these apply to the various organs and functions within the human body.

Astronomy was also part of the astrological tradition at that time, being simply the mathematical branch of the subject. There was no bitter distinction between the two as there is today. Astrology was taught at academic centres throughout the civilised world, united with subjects as diverse as philosophy, music, architecture, politics, agriculture and the arts.

With the decline of Rome and the gradual emergence of the dark ages in Europe, it was the Islamic world that continued the astrological tradition here in the West. It added little of originality, but many of the star names we use today come from it, and the Islamic culture further refined the whole process of observation, compiling more and more accurate tables of projected planetary movements, called ephemerides. Astrology, meanwhile, continued to flourish in India and China, with a growing cross-fertilisation of ideas between East and West taking place in those lands.

With the European Renaissance came perhaps the greatest flowering of astrological inventiveness. Here many branches of the art reached their peak of excellence and popularity. There was still little antagonism between astrology and the Church at this time, and many leading figures in the establishment, including the Pope, understood and welcomed the use of astrology in their own affairs as much as in the secular world. Astrological medicine was taught at centres such as Padua, while in Florence and Rome the blending of classical and humanist ideals, all permeated with astrological lore and symbolism, inspired some of the greatest achievements in the arts and sciences.

Many famous and celebrated figures of the times employed their own astrologers, the fabulous courts of the Medici family, for example, while we know that Elizabeth I of England commissioned the astrologer and scientist Dr John Dee to determine the most propitious date for her coronation. Astrology was used extensively for revealing character, answering questions, locating missing persons or goods, speculating on the course of military campaigns and for judging relationships of all kinds. During the English civil war, astrologers worked with the armed forces of both sides, and one of these, William Lilly, later found himself in considerable trouble with the authorities for predicting the great fire of London in 1666 with such accuracy that many thought he might have had a hand in starting it! Astrology was at its zenith in these times. It touched the lives of all, from the highest of courtiers to the humblest of citizens.

By the late sixteenth century, however, astrology in the

West was in decline. The spirit of the Enlightenment had produced a new-found confidence in man's powers over nature that temporarily eclipsed the by then slightly decadent pronouncements of astrologers. The penny almanacs that were widely distributed at that time on almost every street corner were of highly questionable quality and authenticity, and these did little to endear astrology to the newly emerging intelligensia. Astrology, and particularly astrology as a means of forecasting events, lost much of its intellectual credibility, appearing to be unscientific and outside the normal techniques of experimentation and replication.

The rise of maritime power and commerce, which used the stars for chronology and navigation, and hence for making money, was perhaps an additional factor in the decline, as was the Reformation with its penchant for burning at the stake all witches, and indeed anyone remotely connected with the occult. Astrology went underground for a while, at least until the early nineteenth century. When it did re-emerge it was all the stronger for the experience of examination and stringent re-appraisal that had by necessity taken place.

In our own times, there has been a vast resurgence of interest in the subject and it is today as popular and widespread as ever, not only through the bogus practice of pop astrology, but also among intellectuals and professional people the world over who understand and use serious, chart-based astrology sensibly and prudently to plan and manage their daily affairs.

In our own times much of the emphasis has shifted to a scientific approach and recent research has provided concrete evidence for at least some of astrology's long-cherished traditions. Before looking at modern trends in astrology, however, it might be of interest to consider once again for a moment the long and impressive pedigree that sustains it. For indeed some of the most brilliant and influencial men and women on the stage of world history have studied, supported and encouraged the subject. Here is a by no means exhaustive list of distinguished persons known to have been wholly or partly sympathetic to the subject:

Abelard, Peter; Aeschylus; Albertus Magnus; Alcuin; Alexander the Great; Anaximander; Aquinas, St Thomas; Aristotle; Ashmole, Elias; Augustine, St (later anti); Averroes; Bacon, Francis; Bacon, Roger; Bede, the Venerable; Bernhardt, Sarah; Blake, William; Boehme, Jacob; Botticelli; Boyle, Robert; Brahe, Tycho; Bruno, Giordano; Byron; Caesar, Julius; Cromwell, Oliver; Charlemagne; Charles I of England; Charles II of England; Chaucer; Copernicus; Dante; Dee, John; Dryden, John; Duns Scotus; Durer, Albrecht; Elizabeth I of England; Emperor Augustus; Emperor Claudius; Emperor Domitian; Emperor Hadrian; Emperor Nero; Emperor Tiberius; Emperor Titus; Emperor Vespasian; d'Este, Isabella; Eudoxus; Franklin, Benjamin; Galen; Galileo; Genghis Khan; Goethe; Grosseteste, Robert; Henry VIII of England; Heraclitus; Herodotus; Hesiod; Hipparchus; Hippocrates (later anti); Hitler, Adolph; Holst, Gustav; Homer; Horace; Huygens, Christian; Jefferson, Thomas; Jung, C.G.; Juvenal; Kepler, Johannes; Luther (later anti); Macrobius; Marlowe, Christopher; Mary I of England; de' Medici, Catherine; de' Medici, Cosimo; de' Medici, Lorenzo; Miller, Henry; Milton; Mussolini; Napoleon; Newton, Isaac; Nicolaus of Cusa; Nostradamus; Origen; Philip II of Spain; Plato; Pliny; Plotinus; Pope Alexander IV; Pope Calixtus III; Pope Clement VII; Pope John XX; Pope John XXI; Pope Julius II; Pope Leo X; Pope Paul III; Pope Sixtus IV; Posidonius; Proclus; Pythagoras; Reagen, Ronald; Roosvelt, Theodore; Scott, Michael; Scott, Sir Walter; Schiller; Seneca; Shakespeare; Spinoza; Steiner, Rudolf; Tacitus; Thales; Twain, Mark; Virgil; Vitruvius; Wallenstein.

* * *

MODERN ASTROLOGY: THE SPLIT PERSONALITY

Astrology has always existed at different levels of sophistication. There have always been good and bad astrologers. But today we have an almost schizophrenic state of affairs, with, on the one hand, the advent within the serious astrological community of numerous societies, teaching bodies and research teams of impeccable credentials, while, on the other hand, cheap, purile star-sign columns appear *ad nauseam* in every popular newspaper and magazine, and now even on TV! Never before has the standard been so high, or so low. Astrology now has its clowns and comedians as well as some of its most brilliant researchers and scientists; and not without justification do many now view its treatment within the popular media as little short of a mockery.

This rebirth of astrology, with both its advances and its degeneration, begins around the turn of the century with a growing interest in the subject in North America and Europe, especially in England and Germany. Within this revival certain important figures stand out. For instance, the great Swiss psychologist Carl Jung (1875–1961) was one of the first to recognise the importance of astrological symbolism in the study of the human mind. His concept of archetypes, autonomous forces ever-present in the human unconscious and often appearing as major themes in the arts, mythology and religion, found a natural historical parallel in planetary symbolism. Jung found that certain figures and beings seemed to occur again and again in the dreams, ideas and emotional lives of his patients: the hero type, for example, or the wise old man, the trickster figure, or the earth mother; or universal themes such as wisdom, sacrifice, virgin birth, mystical union of male and female, a flame beneath water, and so on.

All these themes could be found in the mythologies of ancient peoples, and in the classical arts. Yet men and women, often totally without academic knowledge or even basic education, would constantly reiterate these ideas in their dreams or under hypnosis. Often these archetypes of the unconscious, as Jung called them, became driving forces in the lives of perfectly sane individuals as well as those who were mentally disturbed. People were found to be inspired by them, to be influenced by them, and to fear them as well. The archetypes seemed to be something eternal, outliving individual men and women, and it was this that led Jung to the concept of the collective unconscious, something in which all peoples of all ages share, simply by virtue of being alive.

Jung found that the archetypes themselves could best be represented by ancient symbolism. Although superficially it appeared that different cultures at different historical periods enjoyed their own distinctive symbols and metaphors, closer examination proved that certain major themes were repeated throughout, ever-present in the human psyche. The great gods of the ancient and classical worlds, from Mesopotamia through to Greece and Rome, provided the richest sources of symbolism for Jung. Always the gods had shared the same names with the planets: Jupiter, Saturn, Mercury, and so on. And this inspired Jung to study the subject of astrology more seriously. He often approached his patients through astrological symbolism, and also pioneered some experimental research into the astrology of relationships, studying many charts of married couples in search of planetary contacts between the two: 'synastry', as it is called.

Jung, even in his own time, was recognised as one of the foremost scholars of our century. His stature has tended to grow rather than diminish with time, and it was his example that, perhaps more than any other, helped to restore some of the respect that astrology had lost during the eighteenth and early nineteenth centuries.

Since Jung we have seen many landmarks in the progress of astrology: the founding of the Astrological Lodge of London (1917); the American Federation of Astrologers (1938); the Faculty of Astrological Studies (1948) and the Astrological Association of Great Britain (1958), all highly successful bodies that have coordinated and raised the standards of professional practice, teaching and research throughout the world.

Attempts to place astrology on a scientific footing through the use of genuine statistical or experimental evidence has a fairly brief history but one which has accelerated rapidly and impressively during the past forty years or so, culminating in our own times in the thorough, often quite remarkable and brilliant work of men such as Michel Gauquelin and the late John Addey who, in search of demonstrable proof of astrological principles, have examined literally hundreds of thousands of individual charts and subjected these to rigorous analysis. The results of Gauquelin's work during the fifties and sixties, which has since been replicated successfully, have so far proved the most encouraging, already supplying demonstrable proof of at least some of the traditional tennets of astrological lore, namely his 'Mars effect', where this particular body, the planet of stamina and aggression, features more often than chance would normally allow in the charts of eminent sportsmen and women.

Meanwhile, following on from Jung's example, the birth chart has now become a widely used tool within the counselling professions. Many modern astrologers are now qualified psychologists, and many psychologists astrologers. The birth chart of the individual has been found to offer remarkably accurate insights into the often largely hidden and unconscious traits of character and personality. The simple fact that counsellor and patient can sit down together and examine something as objective and as innocuous as an astrological chart on the desk in front of them, has proved to be an excellent point of departure, not only for the discussion of current emotional problems experienced by the patient, but also for revealing any trauma and even illness that might have taken place in the past.

But of course alongside all these wonderfully exciting developments, there has also been in our times an abuse and, to put it not too mildly, a prostitution of astrology perhaps unparalleled in any other period of history. The first regular 'astrological' contribution to appear in the modern press dates from 1930 when an astrological profile on the latest royal baby was run in a popular English newspaper, the *London Daily Express*. This article was so well received that its author, R.H. Naylor, was invited to write a regular column. This was quickly emulated by other papers, all of which quickly realised that lengthy astrological analysis of individuals was far less likely to sell than brief superficial horoscope columns for all. The whole thing went down hill pretty fast and soon became the kind of tittle-tattle we are all familiar with today.

More recently, with the advent of breakfast programmes on TV and radio, there has come the new phenomenon of the show biz astrologer. Such individuals can become household names, followed by millions each morning with a strange mixture of attentiveness, amusement and contempt as they race breathlessly through all twelve star signs in rapid succession during their brief three-minute slot of air time. Yet these people can also be practising consultant astrologers in their own right: working on finished charts for private clients, perhaps all the more successful for such exposure. Maybe, indeed, there is no such thing as bad publicity. Although such glitzy individuals are frequently a source of much grumbling and, to be truthful, not a little jealousy among the serious astrological community, the show-biz astrologer, along with his or her less glamorous cousins in the popular press, appears to be here to stay. From magic to mockery seems a long journey for astrology to have made over the millennia. Yet there is enchantment in laughter, and the ability to make others smile is a quality astrologers should not expel entirely from their ranks if they wish to retain some of the magic.

So by now it should be becoming evident that the answer to our question, 'What is Astrology?' has to be a two- or even a three-fold one. There is the scientific approach, the psychological approach, and the pop version. In order to continue our search it is now time to look at the kinds of astrologers you are likely to encounter in the modern world, and the kinds of astrology they represent.

CHAPTER 4

GOING TO AN ASTROLOGER

The astrologer is a rare breed, often difficult to locate, and equally as difficult at times to comprehend, risking slander, ridicule and misrepresentation to a quite staggering degree to ensure the continuation of the species. Contrary to what many seem to believe, however, astrologers are not particularly eccentric. It is a profession, like any other; there are various standards within that profession, of course, and some higher than others; but by and large its members are intelligent, caring and trustworthy individuals going about their daily business and at the same time helping one or two people as they go.

THE GOOD, THE BAD, AND THE UGLY

There are many different kinds of astrologers at large in the world today, but broadly speaking they can be divided into the following categories:

a) Pop astrologers
b) Low-income professionals or small-business persons
c) Private, semi-professional astrologers
d) Fully professional consultants.

Most people have contact with astrology through newspapers, magazines, TV, or radio. This is the work of the so-called pop astrologers. Let's look at them first.

Pop Astrologers

In truth, these are little more than journalists or show-biz personalities working on a few vague astrological principles to provide mass predictions of a general and superficial kind. When acting in this capacity, they are in the business of entertainment, not astrology, although sadly many if not most people associate the subject with this kind of razzamatazz.

By necessity, no account can be taken of individual character when such predictions are made. The entire population is divided into twelve groups simply by virtue of that part of the year in which their birthdays happened to fall, i.e. Aries: 21st March to 20th April, regardless of time, or place, or actual year of birth, which, as we have seen, are all vital pieces of information in the composition of a proper chart. Fortunately most of us would not act on any of the pronouncements made in articles or programmes of this nature, nor are we intended to. They are there to be enjoyed, and that's all.

The Small-Business Person

With the advent of computer technology, it was perhaps inevitable that sooner or later the small business person would stand up and be counted in the astrological world. These are individuals who may well call themselves astrologers when they advertise for your attention in magazines or through the post; this is rather like your local pharmacist calling himself a doctor of medicine. These people are in business for business sake; they work quickly, using computers for interpretation as well as calculation. The results are usually lengthy and ponderous computer print-outs of personality traits.

The kinds of computer programs they have access to vary greatly in sophistication, and of course much depends on the kind of prices quoted in the advertisements, 'You pays your money, you takes your choice.' By its nature this kind of work is unable to synthesise the various parts of the chart into anything resembling a meaningful whole. Repetitions and contradictions clutter the pages, often leaving the client feeling dissatisfied or confused. He or she may even feel, not without justification, that they have been taken for a ride.

Using whatever birth data you can supply, complete or otherwise, operators of this kind will run off an analysis of your character, perhaps with a rudimentary forecast attached, for a fee corresponding to about one twelfth of the national average weekly wage, or sometimes even less. And although the more up-market versions of these packages can provide the newcomer to astrology with an adequate introduction to the subject, they have little real intrinsic value. The whole thing is conducted on a strictly mail-order basis with no personal contact whatsoever between astrologer and client. Individual factors such as health, environment, relationships and personal aspirations can therefore never be taken into account.

Private, Semi-Professional Astrologers

If value for money is related to the amount of time a fellow human being is prepared to work on your behalf, for little financial reward, then the men and women in this category are worthy indeed. Invariably, they will have studied astrology over a long period of time, either privately or with one of the principle schools. They may often, though by no means always, hold a professional diploma from these schools and be signatories to a code of ethics, an example of which is reproduced on page 50 in Figure 5. They might advertise their services but usually rely on word-of-mouth recommendations. They are also often to be found through the consultants' lists circulated by the schools.

These are men and women of high integrity who take a sincere pleasure in their work. They will insist on full and

FACULTY OF ASTROLOGICAL STUDIES

CODE OF ETHICS

I, the undersigned, wishing to receive the Diploma of the above Faculty, accept without reservation the conditions and propositions set out here, and undertake to fulfil these to the best of my ability.

1. I will endeavour to act at all times in such a way as to enhance the good name of astrology, explaining its true nature as I understand it to all interested persons and defending it against unjust aspersions or ill-informed attacks.

2. I will similarly seek to promote the welfare and good name of the Faculty of Astrological Studies by all appropriate and honourable means.

3. I undertake not to use my Diploma qualification in connection with 'sunsign' forecasting for the media.

4. In all my astrological work, whether professional or otherwise, I will abide by the following rules.

   (a) When undertaking natal work I will explain clearly that unless the time and place of birth can be given with reasonable accuracy any interpretation supplied must be regarded as incomplete or inadequate.
   (b) For all professional work I will charge an adequate fee except in the case of a client who is in genuine need of help but is unable to pay, in which case I will adjust or waive my fee.
   (c) I will make an individual and original study of each case, and will not use any form of duplication; nor will I use the writings of others without due acknowledgement. If a computer analysis forms all or part of my work, I will advise my client in advance, and will give a clear explanation of how it differs from an individual, non-computerised analysis.
   (d) In work stated to be astrological I will not insert anything that is not founded on true astrological science. Should I wish to give advice or information derived from other sources, I will do this separately, making clear to the client that it is not based on astrology.
   (e) I agree to respect strictly all confidences made to me.
   (f) I will not use for my own advantage any knowledge of others gained in the course of my work; nor will I keep for private gain any discoveries I might make which could benefit astrologers generally.
   (g) I will use discretion in making any public statement regarding political matters or persons prominent in public life, and will avoid all such as are contrary to good taste or undesirable in the public interest.

Finally, I admit the right of the Council of the Faculty in the event of wilful or grave violation of this Code of Ethics to withdraw my Diploma and erase my name from the Register of Diploma Holders of the said Faculty.

....
SIGNATURE   DATE

....
WITNESSED

Figure 5.   The Code of Ethics of the Faculty of Astrological Studies

unambiguous birth data, will interpret each client's chart on an individual basis, and will explain their findings carefully and patiently, either in written replies or personally through an informal discussion of the chart itself. A typical assignment, with a general forecast, will require two or three days hard work, and so fees ranging from about one quarter to about one third of the average weekly wage will be quoted. This is actually low-paid work for the amount of hours put in, and some form of additional income is sometimes needed.

Most fully professional astrologers will have served their apprenticeship in this capacity until they have built up a sufficiently large clientelle and a sufficiently consistent track record to be able to rely solely on astrology for an income. Once this is achieved, our dedicated astrologer, for he will be dedicated if he is able to reach such a level, will be ready to graduate into our next and final category: the fully fledged professional, earning, we sincerely hope, a comfortable living at his or her craft.

Fully Professional Consultants

These people rarely if ever advertise. They may be qualified through one of the recognised schools, but may also have been taught privately by other astrologers and may specialise in particular fields such as Natal, Horary or Financial astrology, in which they will have great experience and expertise. Naturally, they will command high fees: anything from around half to several times the average weekly wage for a natal chart alone. Their clients will invariably be wealthy and highly successful professional people or representatives of private institutions. They will sometimes combine astrology with a second profession such as psychotherapy or investment analysis. The demands of discretion and trust placed upon this kind of astrologer are considerable.

In practice there is no clear-cut distinction between those in the last two categories. Often the best astrologers are not the ones that command the highest fees. Also, occasionally, an astrologer from the first catagory will be so well-known and so much in demand as to be able to work also as a fully professional consultant.

DOWN TO BUSINESS

A User's Guide

When you contact a semi or fully professional astrologer, the first thing he or she will want to know is your birth time. We have seen that in order to calculate and draw up a suitable birth chart, the exact time, place, and date are required. If you do not know your exact birth time, the astrologer will probably have one or two useful suggestions as to how this can be ascertained.

The next question the astrologer will probably ask is why you want the work done. What exactly are you looking for? This is because most people when they go to an astrologer for the first time are not aware of the variety of jobs that can be undertaken. For example, astrology is not only about forecasting; many astrologers will confine themselves to character analysis alone. They examine the psychological implications of the birth chart in great detail, the 'personal mythology' of each client, and avoid the area of prediction altogether, believing it to be too unreliable, and believing also that character itself is destiny.

At the great temple of Apollo at Delphi in classical Greece was to be found the following simple inscription, 'Know thyself'. The ideal in natal astrology is to help people to do just that, and thereby encourage the individual to take charge of the present as well as the future. Certainly astrology and counselling blend well in this way, and they are often combined with great success.

Most people, however, are interested in forecasting. They want to know the future trends in their lives, not as an excuse for laziness, but so they can plan for the more positive changes that could be forthcoming, or attempt to avoid the negative ones. Although the birth chart is still the fundamental tool in this respect, predictive work itself is a complex business, and involves far more activity on the part of the astrologer than we have seen so far.

For example, one method of forecasting is based on projections of current daily movements of planets, including sun and moon, onto natal positions. These are called 'transits to the birth chart'. In other words the astrologer must see whether any planetary movements for, say, the year ahead will make cross-aspects to positions in the individual's birth chart.

An example of a transit to a birth chart is shown in Figure 6. The birth chart positions are marked inside the chart wheel,

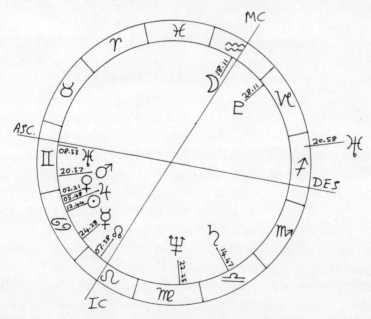

Figure 6. One method of forecasting follows the daily movement of the planets, or 'transits', and relates these to the birth chart. This is a typical example showing transits to such a chart (see text)

while the transitting position for just one planet, Uranus, is drawn on the outside. The most salient cross aspect that Uranus makes on this day is the opposition (180-degree separation) to birth-chart Mars. Mars, as we have seen, is the warrior of the zodiac: aggression, libido, the conquering spirit. Uranus is much less specialised, however: raw energy, chaos and revolution, the starry sky in mythology. Its nature is particularly explosive, violent and unpredictable. As it is an outer planet in our solar system, and therefore a slow-moving body as seen from the earth, this particular aspect can take place only every 84 years. As the opposition of planets is traditionally associated with tension and conflict, one might well expect this to coincide with a rare and unpleasant event.

The birth chart in this case is not that of a person, but of a nation, the USA, based on the time of the declaration of independence in 1776. The position of Uranus was for the morning of 28th January, 1986, and the launch of the ill-fated space shuttle, Challenger, in which the entire crew perished. Dedicated to the furthering of 'star wars' the shuttle mission was a national tragedy which grounded the entire American space programme overnight.

Of course, there are around thirteen fixed points to consider in the natal chart, and ten transitting bodies in constant motion every day. Not only transits, but also eclipses are used in this respect. Some astrologers even use the mid-points between the planets, and aspects to these mid-points, making for literally thousands of possible permutations into the future. This is where the skill and experience of the astrologer comes in, knowing which cross-aspects to reject as much as which ones to accept for the purposes of forecasting.

Perhaps the most widespread method of forecasting uses the 'progressed chart'. This is a separate chart drawn up for each consecutive day after birth, which in turn corresponds to each consecutive year of life in real terms. This day-for-a-year system, as it is sometimes termed, is arguably the practitioner's most valuable tool in predictive work. Again, the astrologer is looking for cross-aspects to the birth chart. If for example Jupiter was in conjunction with the birth-chart sun on the thirtieth day after birth, then one would expect the thirtieth year of life to be coloured by that feature. It might mean, among many other possibilities, a prolonged period of study or intellectual expansion, or a long journey. Mutual aspects between bodies within the progressed chart itself are also considered.

In practice, the progressed positions are often superimposed onto a copy of the birth chart, usually drawn in a different colour, in order to present this to the client in a more agreeable form.

Meanwhile, the actual interpretation can be presented in a variety of ways. Some astrologers stick to written work, others like to see the potential customer first before deciding on the best possible approach to his or her particular inquiry. Still others like to provide the client with a cassette recording of the interview or counselling session. More than anything though, a good astrologer will always take time to listen to what the client has to say, and will tailor the finished work specifically to that individual's needs and temperament.

Here you will often be invited into the home or office of the astrologer so that the qualities, positive and negative, of the chart can be discussed. The tone is invariably friendly and informal, but with frankness and honesty much to the fore. A client should never expect flattery from any astrologer. That would be a waste of time for all concerned. You will, however, have plenty of opportunity to explain your personal circumstances and your aims and ambitions. As with many other forms of professional guidance, this can prove a highly stimulating and rewarding experience.

That one visit, perhaps accompanied by some written work may be all you need, but many clients will return from time to time for regular meetings and up-dates, when more specialised work can be undertaken.

For example astrology can throw considerable light on the often thorny subject of relationships through the comparison of two or more separate birth charts. Again, it is a case of looking for cross-aspects, but this time between bodies in one birth chart and another. By this, one can judge compatibility, shared interests, points of conflict, and so on. This kind of astrology is called Synastry (syn = together; astra = star).

In a romantic relationship, for instance, one is looking for connections between the sun, moon, Mars and Venus, cross aspects from one birth chart to another. One partner might have, say, the sun in a square (90-degree) aspect to the other's moon; or Venus to the other's Mars, and so on. Again there are many possible permutations, and the whole range of human relationships and interactions should be discernable by comparing the other planets in this way.

Highly accurate delineations and forecasts can be achieved using the techniques of Horary astrology, the branch that deals with the answering of specific questions. Accuracy, however, can only be achieved when the client is clear on the information he or she wishes to obtain, and can therefore formulate a precise and lucid question. A chart is then drawn up for the moment the question is asked, the 'birth' of the question, and judged accordingly.

There are many well-documented cases in which horary charting has produced spectacular results. One particularly clever lady I know has the knack of being able to locate lost animals or pets using the tenets of horary astrology. The owner, who might for example have lost his pet cat, simply comes along and asks, 'Where is Tiddles?' Immediately a chart is drawn up for that moment so information can be deduced as to the likely direction, surrounds and conditions in which the animal should be located. And it works!

The hard-nosed world of big business also occasionally takes more than a passing interest in astrology. Astrology has always been employed in the drawing up of what are called Electional charts. These are used for determining the most suitable times for embarking on a business venture, signing a contract, or even laying a foundation stone. Although little used in Europe these days, this kind of astrology is still widespread in the East.

In the West though, astrologers are far more likely to be employed in speculating on economic trends and the fluctuations of stock market and commodity prices. I think the ordinary man in the street might well be astonished by the extent to which astrological counselling contributes to certain shifts in trading sentiment, particularly in the Far East. All the world's great financial centres, London, New York, Tokyo and Hong Kong, have their financial astrologers, whose work must by necessity remain secret much of the time.

So there is plenty of variety and plenty of choice within the profession. But outside this you will also find many many interested amateurs and students of astrology. The subject is now regularly taught at adult education level in most countries in the West, and there are numerous smaller, often more specialised schools springing up everywhere alongside the fast-expanding major ones. Some useful addresses are listed at the end of this book for those who might be interested in studying the subject.

I hope by now to have gone some way towards answering the question: What is Astrology? There is hardly a facet of life that it does not embrace: the arts, sciences, social and political institutions, families, businesses, nations, all are accessible and open to investigation from its point of view. It is above all else a practical and useful subject, providing guidance, information, and an especially creative and dynamic vehicle for self-discovery.

What astrology is not, however, and this might well surprise many of its critics, is fatalistic or dogmatic. At the core of astrological doctrine, particularly in the twentieth century, is the recognition of free will and self-determination as fundamental facts of life.

Like the American Constitution, 'We hold these truths to

be self-evident': liberty, freedom of choice, self-determination. In truth, astrologers and their adherents have nearly always considered the higher or the thinking part of the human being to be absolutely free. Only the lower self, the body, the passions and the senses are subject to natural forces. Whether the stars and planets contain the origins of such natural forces, or whether they are simply indicators of a process common to all, both us and the skies, is of little real consequence. The two happen together, that's all; and changes in us are synchronised with changes in the heavens. This is altogether a highly convenient state of affairs; and it seems only sensible to take advantage.

Astrology is one rather good way of providing information, one more valuable string to the bow. Used intelligently it can be of inestimable value in the turbulent world of human affairs. Astrology is there to be used.

When you go to your friendly neighbourhood astrologer, therefore, do not expect him or her to provide concrete directives for conducting your future. Do not expect a list of the inescapable calamities and golden moments of good fortune that must surely wait in your predestined future. If your astrologer is any good at his or her job, such an approach will never be considered. The astrologer is not a crystal gazer, not a clairvoyant, not a magician. He or she is interested only in facts, and in how these can relate to your existence in the here and now. The astrologer knows that what you become tomorrow is largely a result of how you see yourself today. You will be helped to see yourself accurately. The rest is up to you.

Now having well and truly nailed our colours to the mast it is time to consider matters of survival. Self-defence for astrologers and astrology. Read on.

PART TWO
SELF-DEFENCE

CHAPTER 5
KNOW THE ENEMY

*No matter if professional, amateur or simply an ardent
enthusiast of astrology, each of us with such an interest is likely
to encounter a certain animosity from time to time. Even those
with just a passing interest in the subject can feel intimidated at
times. Why should we astrologers put up with this! Why so
often, whether in a social situation, with family and friends, or
in our day-to-day routine among colleagues or work-mates, do
we passively accept a reaction from others which, when
unfavourable, can range from silent indifference to utter horror
and indignation. All this simply because we have, perhaps
inadvertently, perhaps on purpose, let it be known that we
sympathise with the fundamental astrological tenet that the
movements of the sun, moon and planets, together with the
spatial coordinates of horizon and zodiac, have some form of
correspondence with the lives of individual people here on earth.*

Just suppose that someone has posed those ubiquitous
social questions, 'What do you do? What are your interests
or hobbies? What sort of things do you like reading?'

When the time comes for us to reply we shouldn't baulk
at it. We must be confident that we can back-up our position, that we can relax and enjoy the conversation — to
explain ideas if possible, or defend ourselves and resist
abuse if necessary. In short, it's about time we started
sticking up for ourselves.

Firstly, let us assume that any attack we are likely to
experience will be basically verbal in nature. Thus, you

might be relieved to know, this book stops well short of the point where you will be urged to roll up your sleeves and fight! Nevertheless, it is worth remembering that what holds good for a physical contest often proves relevant in debate.

The first law of self-defence, verbal or physical, is *be aware*. Treat everyone as a potential aggressor. This may sound paranoid, but it need not be so. There is absolutely no need to be tense or withdrawn. Simply be aware that even the most friendly and amicable of individuals can turn nasty at the slightest mention of the word astrology. This normally arises from a deep-seated fear of the irrational and, therefore, of the unconscious — be it his or her own unconscious or the seemingly often violent unconscious promptings of others.

The 'enemy' comes in four main types, corresponding to the four elements of astrology: Fire, Earth, Air and Water. Part of your initial training should be to try, as quickly as possible, whenever you encounter a stranger or are introduced to anyone for the first time, to form an opinion of his or her element. This may not necessarily correspond with their sun sign, of course. The element-balance of an individual reflects the 'whole' person in a way the sun sign can never do. The Chinese and those in the West practising acupuncture, homoeopathy, etc., still use this form of judgement in the diagnosis of illnesses, as did the old European physicians, of course, with their four humours: Choleric, Melancholic, Sanguine and Phlegmatic. Today, many psychologists, especially those who adhere to the Jungian scheme of things, make use of what are called the four functions of consciousness: Intuition, Sensation, Thinking and Feeling.

For those not familiar with this time-honoured approach to evaluating personality and individual temperament, the following table may be helpful. The various systems just mentioned are coordinated under the astrological elements. Study this for a while; read through the following para-

ELEMENT	HUMOUR	TYPE
FIRE	CHOLERIC	INTUITION
EARTH	MELANCHOLIC	SENSATION
AIR	SANGUINE	THINKING
WATER	PHLEGMATIC	FEELING

Note: Phlegmatic can also be applied to Earth, as can Melancholic to Water. They are interchangeable.

graphs, then go out and do a little bit of 'people-watching' and you will be surprised at how quickly you become used to looking at and understanding the world in this way. It can be useful.

We are going to examine each element in turn and later take a look also at some basic defence postures that may be used against each type, especially by the beginner. All these basic postures will stand you in good stead later when you come to sparring and, ultimately, real combat situations, so study them carefully. Naturally, we will assume that in each example the person we are describing is anti-astrology and is expressing the more negative and unpleasant features of his or her element.

Earth

Let us deal first of all with probably the most common adversary you will encounter, the stodgy unimaginative Earth-type. The very proximity of an astrologer or any other person of reasonable sensitivity or imagination is likely at best to furrow their brows, or at worst engender a mild state of apoplexy. Life, for them, is keeping strictly to the routine of working, eating, sleeping and so on. They are the people who have got things 'just about right' while anyone who wastes time on non-profit-making work, devotion or mental exploration, is a fool.

All the negative characteristics of this otherwise excellent element are displayed in attack: indignation, obstinacy, often an aggressive charge from the Taurean bull or Capricorn goat.

Although contrary to his or her own view of themselves, the Earth type is prone, when excited or threatened, to give way to all kinds of irrational fears and to reach instantly for the panacea of dogma and orthodoxy. Do not expect a courteous exchange of views therefore. This type will bellow and grunt its disapproval, shrug its shoulders or simply ignore you altogether. This is also the 'rock', the 'real man', who is terrified of ever appearing vulnerable or eccentric. This can often prove to be an utterly impervious streak: a practicality, a realism amounting almost to a kind of madness. In social terms, the fear is of rejection by the group, and hence deprivation. The material, often greedy nature of the Earth type lives in dread of this.

Water

Generally, the 'feeling type' of person typified by the Water element is likely to be sympathetic to the metaphysical or mystical dimension of life. But remember we are interested only in the version that could prove a potential aggressor, the kind that has had his or her emotional being distorted and twisted back on itself by painful experience.

Water element people have deep feelings; and when they hurt, they hurt badly. In consequence, they are likely to prove the worst and most passionate cynics and sceptics of all. Here you find the bitter Scorpions and Crabs; the totally detached Fishes.

They do like to probe, however, to grub around beneath the surface, to expose all those old wives tales or follies. You can hear them in conversation exploding myths or debunking popular heroic reputations in the way other people might be cracking walnuts.

Example: 'Oh, of course, Francis Drake wasn't playing bowls at all when the news of the Armada came. He was actually in bed asleep — ha, ha! And the only reason we won anyway was because of the appalling English weather.'

Example: 'Well, naturally, the whole motivation behind space exploration is purely military. Romantic notions aside, it all comes down to getting a useful return for your money.'

And inbetween such startling revelations as these you may well detect something like, 'Naturally, anyone with any sense realises there is absolutely no rational or scientific evidence for ESP, divination, astrology or any of those other attractive superstitions.'

You might notice here that the enemy could be fairly articulate, perhaps even quite academic. But do not forget the earlier point that your presence is always likely to tweak at the hidden nerve of repressed feelings. The rationality which, by way of compensation, they strive for so fervently and yet usually stumble over so heavily when put to the test, is likely to desert them at precisely such moments — as if they are fighting for their lives to prove you wrong. Indeed, in some cases they may be doing just that. Feelings can literally kill the moody Water type.

And look out too for the other, less lucid variants: the disgruntled nine-to-five worker, for example. The discovery that you are earning a living, or even a little pocket money, doing something you clearly enjoy could be bitterly resented by anyone stuck in a rut. Watch out for the simmering gaze across a crowded room while he or she eavesdrops on your conversation.

Air

The Air type, if anti-astrology, is the one most likely to view the subject as an insult to his or her intelligence. Air people believe in the power of the brain, and of logic, but they may not be sufficiently aware of the full range and scientific validity of astrology in the light of modern research to be much impressed. And although some Air types could well be absorbed in the study of related subjects such as psychology, fringe medicine, etc., they may still be reluctant to express any kind of commitment.

However, this is the type most open to debate and reasoned argument. They may already be stimulated by the mythology and history of astrology, but — again — prefer to keep this interest at arm's length, rejecting something they might dearly like to believe in. They need to remain logical and reasonable at all times, finding the world of feelings rather incomprehensible and fraught with danger: a kind of self-defence also.

Occasionally, though, you may cross swords with a more superficial type — the Gemini style at its worst and most shallow. Here, the challenge may be swift and fleeting and edged with great wit. This could be even quite cruel and offensive, and you will have to be sharp to keep ahead.

Watch for the barrage of words, the quick repartee.

Fire

You will easily spot the Fire types. They are hard to ignore. When they attack, it may often be unprevoked: aggressive, direct, full steam ahead — a bluster of a sentence such as, 'You don't believe in all that junk, do you!'

Very succinct and to the point, Fire people.

This type, the life and soul of the party, confident and yet dreading that their popularity might ever flag, is best described by the distinctly non-technical, rather unflattering term: the Smart-arse. They may be anything from an utter oaf right through to the saviour-of-the-world type, who feels personally obligated to crusade against darkness and ignorance, or in other words anything that in the least antagonises or threatens the comfortable and cosy world they are proud to rule. This type loves to hand out tips and advice, and loves to be thought of as practical and informed.

Fire types are generally the 'best' people. How do you spot the best people, you may ask? Don't worry: they'll let you know; they usually tell you so themselves. Watch out for the pouting Lions, the zealous Rams. Watch for the flamboyance, the loud voice, those who seem to have an opinion on just about anything. Be prepared, too, for the most outrageous remarks of all from those Sagittarians, who will delight in the most clumsy and ill-timed observations on anything from your political ideology to the colour of your socks.

So much for recognising the enemy. Now it is time to consider our reactions whenever we find ourselves in a tight spot, confronted by someone with a point to make.

CHAPTER 6

DEALING WITH THE BULLY

We have learnt to recognise the types. It is now time to prepare a few important opening moves for use against anyone who is on the offensive. These, and the slightly more advanced blocks in the next section, should be learnt well, almost by heart, so that they will emerge spontaneously or at least seemingly without effort. They will give you time, a vital breathing-space in which to recall the correct combat procedure and muster your more heavy-weight arguments, examples of which will be introduced later in this book. Remember, the 'bully' will almost certainly not have prepared his offensive. If you have at least mastered the basic blocks, you already have the advantage.

Important . . . never, under any circumstances, initiate a confrontation. Remember always that *you* are the secure one. *You* do not need to prove anything to anybody. Never tempt an opening. In conversation never advertise yourself or your interest in astrology. Wait until you are asked. Then distinguish between a polite inquiry and a genuine attack. Never become angry. Never be the first to turn from a peaceful confrontation and give up the struggle. When challenged, meet force with equal force, always by degrees proportional and just a little greater than the force being directed against you and your beliefs.

And remember, too, don't waste time considering the nature of your opponent's sun sign. Simply estimate the element he or she most evinces. Then go for the soft-spot, the one most vulnerable to that element. In other words:

Earth — Hit at the intransigence.
Water — Hit at the jealousies and resentments.
Air — Hit at the indecisiveness.
Fire — Hit at the vanity.

Posture and Attitude

We will now look at some purely defensive stances and preliminary blocks that might be exchanged during any sudden, unprovoked attack. Bear in mind that these are not designed to be devastating, but simply to check your opponent's progress and provide you with the time to prepare a more penetrating counter-attack or, hopefully, develop a proper debate. Against the bully, and for all types — Earth, Water, Air or Fire — there are a few basic rules for posture which must be observed. Initially, as in any normal day to day situation, you should appear open, relaxed and accessible. No matter what the element type, look your opponent straight in the eye, especially when he or she is talking. If tensions are running high, fix your gaze just between the eyes. Try to keep an open, relaxed stance, and avoid fidgeting or grinning too much. This may sound trite, but remember most people will expect you to be an eccentric and will be looking hard for odd traits and mannerisms to confirm their suspicions.

If the exchange is on an equable polite level you may retain this open stance, taking care not to shut yourself off by crossing your arms or legs. Hands in pockets is also rather secretive and unattractive. People like to see your hands. If you are wearing a jacket, keep it unbuttoned. A buttoned-up chest gives the impression of someone closed in and resisting intimacy.

If the confrontation becomes offensive, however, you can start to introduce some rejection postures: legs and arms crossed; hands hidden, just up behind the neck if seated, or behind the back if standing. Searching for something in your pockets, brief-case or handbag, or fixing your eyes on

69

something happening at the other side of the room, are all effective ways of detaching yourself from the conversation. Turning your head away while someone is speaking can have a most disconcerting effect. But remember, it is not a matter of proving that you are right, or to look superior. The moment you feel you are becoming emotionally involved, feeling threatened in any sense by someone's unreasonable aggression, remove yourself physically from the scene — and quickly. In any event, it should certainly be beneath your dignity to indulge in a slanging match. The great Chinese classic the Tao Te Ching has something interesting to say on this topic.

> He who knows does not speak;
> He who speaks does not know.
> He who is truthful is not showy;
> He who is showy is not truthful;
> He who is virtuous does not dispute;
> He who disputes is not virtuous.[1]

So, here are a few examples of evasions and parries, cut-off remarks designed to neutralise the bully and to finish the exchange quickly. These are listed according to the element type against which they are the most effective. They are interchangeable of course and you can easily adapt them to your own situation.

The Stroppy Earth Types

This is never an easy kind to defend against, often because the attack takes place when your back is turned. Humour and wit should be employed, as well as a certain nonchalance. Don't let yourself appear too concerned. This is especially valuable in a social situation, thereby threatening your opponent with a sense of alienation. You will need to square up to this kind of individual, while remaining at all times respectful. Keep your head erect and, if seated, your hands together, fingers pointed. This creates the impression of calm self-confidence. It is also the pose of the specialist or expert, or of the teacher in the face of a quarrelsome child. It threatens a kind of parental disapproval and subsequently — most dreadful of all to Earth types, remember — deprivation. If things get nasty, try a quick side step such as:

'Astrology, of course, doesn't have all the answers. That's why it rarely appeals to people who already believe they do.'

Here you are touching the raw nerve of the Earth type: complacency. This will usually work, but it could, in rare circumstances be inflammatory. Once the genuinely disgruntled Earth type has expressed disapproval of your existence and appears to be squaring up for a real onslaught, often voiced in the form of a grunt or a snort or two, respond with a rapid body swerve such as:

'I think we can at least agree that there is no point in coming to blows over it, don't you?'

He or she will, in fact, probably quieten down instantly and agree that this sounds reasonable enough. Earth types do respect reason. But if not . . . run.

The Emotional Water Type

In eye-ball to eye-ball conversation with Water people it is always advisable to be prepared for the worst, which in this kind of situation can be vicious irony and cynicism. And although with the more genteel types you can attempt to draw them into a discussion, remember that he or, more rarely she, is basically a person who does not wish to be seen to yield. They were once idealists before disappointments and misfortune turned them in on themselves. And nothing is more unreasonable than a frustrated idealist. When repressed feelings are on the line, the Water types can become hysterical in their criticism. A simple defensive

71

block on your part could in rare circumstances spark off a vicious counterattack that could be tearful or even down right brutal.

If standing, cross the arms. This is a 'shutting-out' gesture. Look sympathetically but distantly upon their ravings; ignore their tantrums. You are 'not going to love baby', and this is like armour against their brooding displeasure and narrowness which will be evident to all if you draw them out. Then, a gentle warding off manoeuvre can be used such as:

'I'm sorry to see that this encounter upsets you so much.'

This is likely to either throw them entirely off balance or else initiate a swift counter-thrust to the effect of how utterly unconcerned they are — not at all upset, etc., etc. You can deflect this easily with something like:

'Oh, I see — you're always that colour, are you?' referring to a real or absent blush. Worried that they are exposing too many feelings, they will probably soon shut up. Make a pact with them not to drag emotion into the argument. You remain always the person of reason, therefore. They simply make fools of themselves.

All a little 'below the belt' perhaps, but don't worry. If your conscience bothers you, there is another equally efficient way to deal with the situation. This is simply to show your feelings: in fact you can be quite free and unreserved in this. Press back against your antagonist with something like, 'Would you excuse me, please. I find this all rather unnecessary and distressing. I hope you can understand.' And then make your exit, looking a little saddened by the whole affair.

This will take your opponents aback. It may actually make them feel rather ashamed; and they will not pursue you further, unless to apologise. Strange as it may seem, this is a tactic which can turn an enemy into a friend for life! Water types understand emotion and respect deep feelings. They know how easily it is to be hurt and will regret having made such a bad impression on a stranger.

The Talkative Air Types

The intellectual, loquacious Air type is often a pleasure to deal with — that is of course providing he or she is in a good mood. Their challenges are likely to be mild and edged with curiosity, though the bully among this type could be extremely sarcastic and quite humorous as well.

Keep a direct and steady gaze and, if seated, allow the occasional gesture of attentiveness to appear, letting the fingers grip the chin, or tilting the head slightly to one side. Show respect for the other's intelligence, but make it obvious that you consider yourself their equal, and be ready to respond with a few well-placed examples of astrology's uses, concentrating on practical results, statistics, etc. (the kind of thing you will find later in this book).

The really offensive types are harder to handle, and if really psyched-up, the satirical Air type can simply disintegrate an opponent under a laser-sharp beam of wit and cynicism. Much of this will be genuinely brilliant and quite funny. In a social situation, you can expect to be the brunt of endless gibes and wisecracks which can, it must be said, make you into something of a laughing stock.

Your best line of defence, if it is a genuinely witty attack, is to laugh along with it. Don't hold yourself in or appear to take yourself too seriously. This type takes nothing seriously and has a way of making stiffness and formality look ridiculous. Keep your head erect, and foster a slightly ironic gaze. If seated, let your hands drift behind your head occasionally, as though you are enjoying it all immensely. Then, once your opponent has rolled off a particularly corney or hackneyed remark, respond with a good swift jab such as:

'If I were you I'd put that one back in the Christmas cracker where you found it.'

This may well hit a soft spot, since Air types like to see themselves as original and clever. Your remark makes their humour look rather stale, and you are now back in control of the situation. But if the exchange does become bitter, as it easily can with the more determined kind of opponent, start to retreat and back off immediately. Execute a wide sweep or trip, such as:

'Listen — if ever you'd like to discuss this subject in a proper spirit of courtesy, let me know. And if ever I need a comedian for anything, I promise I'll give you a call. OK?'

By this time of course you should be well on the way to removing yourself physically from the vicinity. If they call after you, smile and hold your hand to your ear — you didn't quite catch what they said, and you're not really bothered anyway.

The Impassioned Fire Types

By all appearances the most formidable, the Fire type, is in fact the easiest to keep at arm's length. It's mostly all bluff and bravado when they attack. You, on the other hand, will be ready to respond with some direct blocks and counter-moves, as described in the next chapter; in the meantime, keep up the banter, using mostly monosyllables. Your opponents will soon have wasted a lot of energy, as well as all their best gags, and probably attracted a fair degree of attention from other people nearby in any social situation.

Keep hands linked behind your back in a control posture. You are not having any of it, and you are not in the least impressed. And if you are seated during any of this, try an upwards arm stretch whilst reclining. Yawn or communicate sympathy or feelings of tedium while gazing at others in their company. They are almost certainly as bored as you are by all the histrionics, and at this stage the insecure macho type can be demolished easily with a swift, outspoken thrust, such as:

'Excuse me, would you mind just moving your charisma a little to one side so I can see if there's anything interesting happening over there.'

Alternatively, ask him a question like, 'I bet you're the kind of guy who's into fast cars instead, eh?' Almost certainly the reply will be yes. 'I wish you'd get into one now,' you add.

Meanwhile, the more purely aggressive, usually inebriated individual can be safely allowed to continue, especially in a social situation, plunging further into more and more advanced states of desperation until even they realise they are making a complete idiot of themselves. You can then laugh it off, if you are confident you can make it sound genuine, and turn your attention to other things, perhaps sharing your amusement with a glance at someone nearby. Also, if you feel you can get away with it, try a few dismissive aside jabs, such as, 'Who's your friend?' or 'He's not with you, is he?'

People in the group will probably be so embarrassed by your opponent's poor behaviour by this time that the enemy will become completely isolated, and might even skulk away to lick their wounds elsewhere. He or she is not likely to ever speak to you again, incidentally, so you will have no further bother.

Actually, Fire types are quite often forthright and open, and like to think of themselves as honest too. So, if your antagonist is not being too objectionable, simply use this word 'honest' in a quick cut-off remark — something like:

'Let's be honest, there's not much point in you and I talking about this subject, is there?' And this will often work immediately. Peace returns.

So much for the casual bully, who will only ever attack within a social or group situation: showing off. This is their own little system of defence too, of course, for, as in all walks of life, the bully is only a coward with a fierce countenance. However, we will need shortly to get to grips with some basic blocks: lightweight arguments that can be used in our own and astrology's defence whenever a genuine approach is made. This is what we will be looking at next.

CHAPTER 7
BASIC BLOCKS

The following defensive moves are designed to enable you to resist spontaneous challenges and subsequently to embark upon a strong penetrating counteroffensive. We have already learnt how to deal with the bully; so at this stage we will assume your opponent to be reasonably positive in the use of criticism; able and willing to discuss ideas and exchange opinions intelligently.

Speed is of the essence, as in any combat scenario but do not worry if you are initially slow. If you learn the blocks well, they will come out spontaneously and instinctively with practice. This is vital because, if quick and firm, a well-placed block can put your opponent totally off balance. To be effective it will be a short sentence or two delivered immediately the attacker makes the first real move, without allowing them time to gain the upper hand. Meanwhile, you should have established the element type you are dealing with and adopted the relevant posture. Remember the basic rules: arms away from chest, never folded; feet a little apart, and look your opponent straight in the eye as often as necessary to make your point.

Typical opening attacks with suitable defensive statements now follow, and here I shall present two variations of defence: firstly, an all-purpose block, one that can be used for general use by just about anyone no matter how slender your commitment to astrology, and secondly a more specialised version, pitched more to the needs of the working astrologer. In time you should be able to adapt and combine these blocks to defend against many different lines of attack.

A) 'An Astrologer! Really, you don't believe in all that stuff, do you?'

All-Purpose Block: 'Certainly I do. It's helped me on many occasions to make important decisions . . . and to avoid making a fool of myself.'

Specialist Block: 'Of course! I wouldn't expect to earn a living at something I didn't believe in.'

Note: both these replies demonstrate the free-will emphasis of modern astrology. You are seen as a person of action, someone who puts astrology to constructive use. The all-purpose block also suggests in a subtle way that the opponent might be appearing foolish.

B) 'Astrology! Oh, I always read mine in the newspapers. It never comes true.'

All-Purpose Block: 'Well, if you believe everything you read in the papers, you deserve what's coming to you.'

Specialist Block: 'I'm not surprised. That's not astrology — that's journalism.'

Note: these two can be linked up to form a double block which can be very effective. Judge the ferocity, or otherwise, of the attack and react accordingly.

C) 'Emm . . . Actually, I believe people make their own luck.'

All-Purpose Block: 'That's right, people do make their own luck. And astrology is concerned with what makes people make their own luck.'

Specialist Block: 'Yes, the first thing any reputable astrologer would impress on you is the importance of free choice. Astrology is a bit like the weather forecast. The experts can tell you if it's likely to rain or not — but it's up to you to take an umbrella.'

D) 'Hey! This guy's an astrologer!' (A group situation, this.)

All-Purpose Block: 'Don't worry, it's not contageous. And it rarely proves fatal.'

Specialist Block: 'Yes, I'm fortunate to be able to earn a living doing something I thoroughly enjoy.'

Note: both these blocks are a bit cheeky, and can easily unsettle your opponent. But don't feel guilty. This person is, after all, probably trying to unsettle *you*, at least to begin with. Remember it is essential to remain calm and cheerful when speaking. Don't become snooty.

E) 'Astrology — really! How extraordinary! (The patronising type.)

All-Purpose Block: 'Not really all that extraordinary. Just a rather useful hobby, that's all. One more string to your bow.'

Specialist Block: 'Well, it has been around since about 3000 BC. I'd have thought most people were used to us by now.'

Note: these present the astrologer in a cheerful ordinary light, a visage which will undoubtedly surprise such an opponent, who probably expects you to have at least two heads and a magic wand tucked under your arm.

F) 'Astrology! You're not serious, are you?'

All-Purpose Block: 'Well, I'll be serious if you'd like me to. But we don't need to get too up-tight about it all, do we?'

Specialist Block: 'Well, when you spend at times twelve hours a day, seven days a week doing something, it's rather difficult not to take it seriously. Luckily, it's a particularly interesting job, and also a lot of fun.'

Note: these make the opponent appear rather an oaf, as indeed he probably is. Rest assured, in a social situation you will not have been the only person to have noticed it. Most people prefer someone with a smile on their face; and it's easy, therefore, to make this sort of adversary appear tedious, and thus gain the upper hand.

G) 'Oh well, yes, I'm sure it works out sometimes, this astrology business. But that's just coincidence in my view.' (Coincidence is a favourite word among cynics. But it's an easy one to deal with.)

All-Purpose Block: 'Calling something a coincidence doesn't explain why it happens. I like to know why things happen, and when they are most likely to happen again.'

Specialist Block: 'Yes, it does work out, and frequently. As for coincidence, well, that's just a word, meaning two things that happen together at the same time: *co-incident*. The word itself doesn't get you any closer to explaining what takes place. In fact you are using coincidence as a kind of magical incantation. Whisper this word and, you seem to imply, there is no longer any need to wonder about life's mysteries. That's just pure mental laziness. Astrology, on the other hand, is interested in what lies behind the words, the reality of how things relate.'

Note: unfortunately, many people who use the word 'coincidence' freely will find it almost impossible to understand these arguments; but your blocks will possibly make your opponent feel rather lazy and shallow, and you will at least appear the more broad-minded and thoughtful competitor in any such encounter.

H) 'Astrology! Good heavens, surely you must realise . . . Do you really not understand . . .' (And they will then go on, and on, and on.)

Occasionally you will be unfortunate enough to encounter this kind of 'informed' person who might astonish you by a sudden onslaught of words, a kind of instant vehemence, as though being introduced to an astrologer had suddenly released years of pent-up indignation and resentment. They will prattle on about everything and anything, from the opinions of respected scholars and scientists to their own passionate misgivings on superstition and fatalism: in short everything and anything except astrology itself! Let them have their say, most of which will be unintelligible, and then . . .

All-Purpose Block: 'Could you just repeat that please while I take notes.'

Specialist Block: 'I see. But tell me, do you know anything at all about the profession of astrology? I mean, have you studied the procedure: how it works, where it's applied and what exactly it's used for?'

To which you will receive the inevitable:

'Well no, not really, but . . .'

Don't let them continue after the but. Simply nod your head and say, 'Oh, I see.' Then turn slightly to one side, losing complete interest in them. The result can be devastating, and you may need to adjust the level of your indignation a little if you feel your opponent might, after all, become interested in a genuine discussion.

Note: both these answers, in their own way, will show you in a position of self-control and good humour: an ideal state to maintain at this stage of any encounter.

I) 'Astrology . . . Oh, well I'm not really all that sure if I believe in stuff like that. Hope you don't mind.'

Here we have the typical indecisive type: the kind who normally has to have their opinions made up for them. Look out for the latest fashions in dress or the folded newspaper under the arm.

All-Purpose Block: 'Not at all. Actually, I'm very broad-minded about that sort of thing.'

Specialist Block: 'Oh, that's all right. Neither was I until I studied the subject for myself. I gave it a fair trial, and was rather impressed. It was soon after this that I decided to study it in earnest, and make it my profession.'

Note: the all purpose block here highlights your antagonist's evident lack of broad-mindedness, a fault which you are likely to encounter in almost every opponent. This particular block is well worth learning, therefore, and you can employ it quite freely at any time and in almost any situation.

J) 'Astrology . . . no, surely you mean astronomy, don't you? Well, I'm amazed, frankly, that someone like yourself should take that sort of thing seriously.'

Here it is apparent that you have already made a good impression on your opponent, and he or she is stunned to discover you are concerned with astrology — evidently something with which they have little positive experience. This surprise is, naturally, to your advantage and you can force your opponent to trip up quite easily.

All-Purpose Block: 'Yes, astro' with a logos. That's it. Actually you don't have to commit intellectual suicide to believe in astrology: only take a few risks. In other words you have to dispense a little with the mental routine and be prepared to look afresh at the serious side of the subject. Then I think you'll be impressed. Most people are.'

Specialist Block: 'Well, most of my clients are intelligent, honest professional people, and they certainly take it seriously. Then perhaps they're lucky enough to have been introduced to genuine astrology from the start and realise that the stuff in the newspapers, which is what you probably have in mind, is not at all representative of the subject.'

K)   'Huh! All that sort of thing is just pure escapism, in my view, a search for mystery and excitement: compensation for people who don't already have it in their lives. That's all there is to astrology and things like that.'

Here is another one of those down-to-earth types who love their grub (chips on the shoulder with everything), and who pride themselves on their sense of 'realism'. For them, astrology is inextricably linked with things like Aunt Mary's seance on a Saturday night, and paperbacks on UFOs, and the Bermuda Triangle, while mystery, imagination and excitement are actually qualities belonging more to the pleasures of career, money and the occasional safari holiday. Easy to tackle.

All-Purpose Block: 'So what's wrong with a little mystery and excitement! These are realities that we all need in our lives: sources of inspiration and renewal. Surely you don't believe there can be anything wrong in such valuable and enormously entertaining sensations! We're all of us alive, after all . . . aren't we?'

Note: a little edge of doubt and irony on the final words here can work wonders.

Specialist Block: 'To say that astrology just deals with mystery and excitement is like telling a doctor that he deals only with worry and hypochondria. Astrology is a complete and thorough profession, dealing with ideas, concepts and actions of which you clearly have not the slightest comprehension.'

You will have noticed that so far our blocks have been mild in nature. Dignity and calm are qualities that will always restrain unwarranted aggression, even when your arguments are below their possible best. Remember, a sharp tongue and a dull mind usually go together. You do not deserve to be thought of in this way; so remain polite.

Having said this, it is sometimes useful to be able to counterattack with vigour, to put in a few quick jabs to interrupt the thrust of any reproach or attempted rebuttal that comes your way. The knack of knowing when and how to jab and harry your opponent is easily learnt. For example, listen out for certain key words. If the words 'justify' or 'justice' are used, i.e. 'I can't see any justification for astrology,' you respond with something like, 'It's a poor judge who reaches a verdict without knowledge of all the facts.'

If he or she criticises but won't listen, or tells you they already understand enough to dismiss the subject, you hit back with, 'Surely, no one is qualified to dismiss something he is not willing to have explained or put to the test', *or*, 'You mean you already know enough to sustain your opinions. Surely hardly sufficient to dismiss a subject having the range and antiquity of astrology!'

If the word 'pessimism' is used or pessimism expressed about ever finding anything of value in astrology, you come back with, 'True. Pessimists rarely make the discoveries that optimists make, nor have as much fun making them.'

If, after the initial approach, your opponent suddenly turns away stating angrily that it's just a waste of time discussing such nonsense, you should agree, and then counter straight away with, 'There can only be losers all round when reason has to pit itself against emotion.'

In these replies, always stress your opponent's possible prejudgement of the matter. This prejudgement will almost certainly be the case, for — as you will see from the wealth of evidence for the acceptance or at least the sober consideration of astrology that appears later in this book — there are absolutely no excuses for your opponent's disapproval other than varying degrees of ignorance, and this is even more so if he or she is behaving badly. In fact the worse the behaviour the easier it is for you to reveal and exploit the unsteadiness of their entire stance.

Remember, both justice and hard evidence are on your side. Two formidable weapons. Use them.

CHAPTER 8

INTRODUCING
THE FORM

*In the next two chapters we are going to move beyond the
simple blocks and parries used in the average social situation,
and look towards real discussion and argument: offence and
counteroffensive. The subject covers such a vast field that we will
need a system to help us. Therefore we will explore, one by one,
the twelve basic kinds of critique most often targeted
against astrology.*

Collectively, the twelve following sections could be viewed
as a kind of 'form', a term borrowed from the ancient
Chinese art of Tai Chi Chuan. The form is used in training,
and describes a continuous flow of defensive and counteroffensive moves executed slowly and in a relaxed fashion. The
set order helps with memorising, though in real life, in
debate as much as in combat, one improvises.

It is important to remember that in the event of a real
debate you will need to build up the strength of your
position by degrees. In other words never use your best
argument at the beginning. It may be unnecessary to do so,
and also way above the head of your opponent. This is why
the form appears twice, because we are going to examine
each critique on two different levels. Firstly, we will be
looking at sparring, or argument conducted at a fairly lightweight conversational pace. Then, later on, we take each
encounter onto considerably higher ground, real combat,
where your opponent is likely to be tenacious or using
debate of a fairly heavyweight intellectual class, either in
conversation or by way of correspondence.

THE FORM

Critique		Sparring *Chapter 8*	Combat *Chapter 9*
Critique 1	Pop Astrology	page 87	page 95
Critique 2	Twins	page 88	page 98
Critique 3	Earth-Centred	page 88	page 101
Critique 4	Nations and Peoples	page 88	page 106
Critique 5	Zodiac	page 89	page 110
Critique 6	New Planets	page 89	page 117
Critique 7	Conception	page 90	page 121
Critique 8	Fatalism	page 90	page 126
Critique 9	Forced Births	page 91	page 130
Critique 10	Paganism	page 92	page 134
Critique 11	Influence	page 92	page 142
Critique 12	Relevance	page 93	page 152

The table above shows the form: the twelve types of critique, together with the page numbers where each appears and where you can locate firstly the sparring, and then the combat procedure for dealing with each one. Just about any kind of attack will fall into one of these categories but as the discussion develops you may need to draw upon more than one to maintain your position and, ultimately, to win the argument.

We have already dealt adequately with the impolite or sarcastic opponent, and it is assumed from now on that there is real value in pursuing a discussion and presenting a genuine defence of astrology. In this, therefore, as with all the higher levels of martial arts, we should cultivate a deep and natural respect for our opponent and avoid all bitterness, resentment and innuendo. From now on your tone of voice should be firm but also sympathetic. For remember, the greatest force operating against astrology today is not hostility but ignorance. Your task, therefore, is not only to defend but also to reassure and to educate others.

The form is always practised slowly and calmly. In this way concentration, patience and modesty are developed, qualities every bit as important as fighting skills. In sparring and real combat you should also remain calm at all times. Self-control is the greatest asset, and the most powerful weapon you can ever possess.

SPARRING

The twelve types of critique appear here now in the order of the form as shown in the table on p. 86. Simple but effective defensive responses are shown for each one. Remember to keep your arguments lightweight. There is nothing to be gained here in overcoming your opponent at this stage. This is the essence of sparring.

Critique 1: Popular Astrology

'Astrology can't work. There are only twelve star signs and yet about forty-eight million people in Britain. You can't tell me that a twelfth of the population have the same horoscope.

Sparring: 'You're talking about pop astrology, the stuff you read in newspapers or see on TV. They do the best they can, but it's not real astrology: it's journalism, show business. A professional astrologer will want to know the exact time and place you were born, as well as your birth date, so he or she can calculate what is called a birth chart, a detailed map of the sky that applies to you alone. Only then will an attempt at making predictions be made.

'Naturally this facet of journalism is a constant source of embarrassment to genuine astrologers. At times they have tried to change their image, calling themselves cosmobiologists or astral scientists. But most astrologers find these terms rather pretentious and realise that they only serve to confuse the public.'

Critique 2: Twins

'If the birth time is so important for astrology, what about twins? Some twins are born within minutes of each other, but lead different lives. One twin might even die young while the other lives on to a ripe old age. This shows astrology can't work.'

Sparring: 'Even a few minutes can make a lot of difference to a birth chart. That's why all reputable astrologers insist on working with as accurate a birth time as possible. Twins may not always share the same characteristics, of course, but their lives do generally develop at a similar pace. The differences when they occur are subtle ones, which is exactly what astrology would expect. Even in your example, where one twin dies while the other lives, clearly the same event, namely death, has entered both lives at the same time. One twin dies, while the other is touched radically by the sorrow and tragedy of the death of the other. Surely this is an argument for, rather than against astrology.'

Critique 3: Earth-centred

'Doesn't astrology and all that stuff still put the earth at the centre of the universe? It's centuries behind the times.'

Sparring: 'Not at all. Astrologers, like most educated people, realise that the earth is a planet which revolves around the sun. It's simply more convenient to chart astronomical positions as they appear from the earth because, after all, it's right here that we all have to live. Astrology is concerned with people; people live on the earth.'

Critique 4: Nations And Peoples

'What about when there is a catastrophe involving hundreds of people. Or wars. Would all the people who died in the Hiroshima bomb have had the same fate written in their stars?'

Sparring: 'There are of course astrological charts for nations as well as for individual people. There are charts for governments, great historical events, and so on. In fact, the study of these is one of the oldest forms of astrology, called Mundane Astrology. Naturally, any individual life takes place within this greater framework. I would have thought this was obvious enough. It is especially important to astrologers, who are conscious of such questions.'

Critique 5: Zodiac

'Isn't the zodiac just a line-of-sight effect? The stars in each sign are all different distances from us, aren't they, and not connected in any way? It isn't real.'

Sparring: 'Well, yes, the zodiac is composed of stars at different distances, just as a landscape painting is made up of separate elements at different distances, the trees and hills and so on. The picture is a reality in its own right of course; so is the zodiac.

'The modern astrologer's zodiac is something different again, though. You are probably confusing this with the actual constellations, the old imaginary pictures in the sky. The modern zodiac has more to do with the relationship of the earth in its orbit about the sun than with actual groups of stars. In one form or another this kind of zodiac has been around for a long time. The Egyptians had it; the Greeks had it. Hundreds of generations have come and gone; people like you and me have lived and died but the zodiac is still there. If that's not real, I don't know what is!'

Critique 6: New Planets

'Science has come up with new planets, though, hasn't it? It changes the whole system. Astrologers can't ignore that, can they?'

Sparring: 'No, nor would they wish to. Astrologers do in fact welcome the discovery of planets such as Uranus, Neptune and Pluto. They help enormously in the business of character analysis and prediction. Incidentally, astrologers in England had already named and anticipated the existence of Pluto some twenty years before its actual discovery by the astronomers in 1930.'[1]

Critique 7: Conception

'Astrologers rely on birth times for their work. But surely it's the moment of conception, when all our genetic characteristics come together, which marks the beginning of the individual existence?'

Sparring: 'Actually the old astrologers used to set up conception charts as well. Precise formulae existed for calculation, but naturally no one could ever confirm whether they were correct. The relevance of birth charts, on the other hand, has been confirmed through centuries of continued use. In any case, even the geneticists admit that there is a lot more goes into the making of a human being than just inherited characteristics. Astrology deals with the whole, the emerging individual at the time of birth.'

Critique 8: Fatalism

'I'm my own man: I'm not subservient to anything or anyone. I don't need any astrologer to tell me how to live, or what to do.'

Sparring: 'Right you are! Telling someone how to live is the last thing any reputable astrologer would want to do. But it's worth bearing in mind that even the best of us are subservient to our passions and ambitions at times. Astrology can shed some light on these, while recognising all the time that each person is a totally free and independent being, capable of making his or her own decisions.'

RS.P.

Critique 9: Forced Births

'These days, there's hardly any such thing as a natural birth. Babies are forced, held back or induced so much. Doesn't this somehow throw astrology out?'

Sparring: 'Not in the least. A birth time is a birth time, no matter what circumstances surround it. Everyone is born at the right time, regardless of our fussy little mechanisations in hospitals and nursing homes. On balance, however, astrologers do disapprove of induced births, since there is strong statistical evidence to suggest that this destroys the natural affinity between parent and child.'[2]

Critique 10: Paganism

'Astrology is a wicked, pagan superstition. As a Christian, one naturally believes that God has endowed mankind with free will. To consult the planets about the future is a primitive, heathen practice.'

Sparring: 'On a popular journalistic level, it may seem so. However, real astrology has always recognised the dominance of individual free will. Apart from that, there are many astrologers who are also practising Christians. Even those who are not have absolutely no desire to encourage worship of pagan gods, Jupiter, Saturn, and so on. Rather, they use these bodies to represent psychological or spiritual forces. The blend of Christianity and astrology has a long history, as well. Many of the founding fathers of the Church, for example, were sympathetic to astrology, recognising its importance in both the Jewish and Neo-Platonic traditions from which Christianity derived inspiration.'

Critique 11: Influence

'How can the planets have any effect on us! I've never felt anything. You can't tell me that a few lumps of rock and gas millions of miles away can exert any kind of influence.'

Sparring: 'Well, they do. Influences from such distances are being recorded all the time. Astronomical phenomena effect everything from the quality of radio transmissions to the degree of haemorrhages during surgical operations.

'Anyway, astrologers can get along quite comfortably without the need for influences. For example, farmers will tell you that the swallows invariably leave early before a hard winter, long before any change in the weather that might suggest what is to come. The birds' migration doesn't influence the cold winter any more than the movements of the planets need to influence you and me. They happen together, that's all, and if we use our experience we can draw some useful conclusions about the future.'

Critique 12: Relevance

'Astrology is just old hat, isn't it! It's like religion: people are too smart these days to be taken in by magic and superstition.'

Sparring: 'Perhaps it's not so important in your life, or amongst the people you know, but take my word for it, astrology is still as widespread and popular today as ever. Astrology has nothing to do with magic either, and has plenty of modern practical uses, everything from career planning to stock-market speculation. Yes, it does have a spiritual dimension. Most of the really worth-while things in life do. This does no harm, and can do a lot of good.'

So much for sparring, in which our replies have been kept deliberately brief and rather superficial. However, it is assumed from here on in that your adversaries will be equipped with a moderate knowledge of astronomy and general science. Arming yourself in turn with these really not too daunting technicalities can no longer be avoided, since the subject must be thoroughly understood, and this understanding maintained in an up-to-date fashion if you are to take on any of the really heavyweight challenges that we are going to meet with next.

This book will help you but if you are not yet confident of this level of understanding, then your local library will be able to supply you with a good general background on the kind of topics covered in the form — astronomy, biology, the arts, comparative religion, and so on — all areas touched on by astrology to some extent. Often, even the most esteemed of professional astrologers are found sorely lacking in this kind of knowledge, and so everyone is urged to brush up on the technical side of the subject as soon as possible, otherwise your arguments will be flawed and your entire stance vulnerable to anyone already well versed in these fields.

CHAPTER 9
COMBAT

This is the second, more advanced version of the form. Each critique is treated at considerable length, and obviously you are not intended to memorise every word, nor would this be of much use anyway. As previously mentioned, the separate elements have to be employed creatively and matched to the demands of the moment. Also the full extent of each reply is not likely ever to be needed in the general conversational situation. What is presented here is somewhat of an ideal: two people addressing each other courteously in a quiet room with lots and lots of time to spare. Does this ever happen! However, it is possible you will wish to employ a larger amount of the material in correspondence, in which case you will be able to amend it with whatever latest research is at hand. But note . . . the basic framework of each section has been carefully structured for maximum effect, and this plan of attack should still be of use even when you wish to make extensive changes and additions of your own.

At all times do not lose sight of the basic principles outlined in previous chapters. Stance and attitude remain as important during real combat as they are during the casual opening of the encounter. Relaxation should also not be lost. This is vital. Yield when necessary; be firm when you need to.

You must of course expect interruptions which may break your concentration and tempt you to interrupt back. Ultimately this can only result in an argument or a slanging match and must be avoided by making it clear that you have no wish to discuss the subject in anything other than a calm and sensible manner. No one will ever blame you for wanting to treat the debate seriously, certainly not at this level, but any hint of impatience or hysteria will cast a shadow of doubt over even the finest of speakers.

So, let us recommence the form: each critique appears in the same order as in the previous chapter on sparring, and as shown in the table on page 86.

Critique 1: Popular Astrology

'Although I appreciate the distinction between pop astrology and the professional work which treats each person individually, the fact that the same language and terminology is shared by both types of astrology, suggests that they must also share the same principles. If newspaper astrology is nonsense, how can the other version practised by the esteemed professional be anything more than refined nonsense?'

Note: here it is obviously going to be necessary to explain some of the basic principles of real astrology. There is a lot to tell, of course, but don't become too involved or worry if you leave things out. Your explanation here should be styled merely to demonstrate the complexity of the subject. Unless you and your opponent have a fair smattering of astronomical knowledge, such a task would be futile in any case. Keeping this in mind, proceed along the following lines:

Combat: 'Genuine astrology is not a refinement of pop astrology, as many people seem to think. Pop or newspaper astrology is a wholly modern, and entirely degenerate off-shoot of the mainstream profession. Having appeared as recently as the 1930s, it draws on one small working principle from the vast range of astrological practice, namely the sun signs of its readers, in order to make a few general sweeping pronouncements. These are, in any case, couched in such nebulous terms as to be virtually meaningless.

'To explain why popular astrology is such a debasement of the real thing, requires a little technical understanding of the subject. To begin with, simply knowing the birthday of someone is of no use whatsoever to any serious astrologer. Rather, precise and complete data is needed, including year, time and place of birth, in order to plot the positions of the sun, moon and planets onto a detailed map called a birth, or natal chart. This process will also reveal many additional factors such as the ascending and culminating degrees of the ecliptic for that locality, and the actual house system of the chart derived from those points.

'Any number of these features can be activated by current, day to day movements in the heavens called transits. Not only this, but movements shortly before and shortly after birth are also taken into account in a complex business of forecasting called progressions. So, to produce a satisfactory forecast for any one year, for example, a genuine professional astrologer specialising in this field will need to spend perhaps two or three days, firstly on calculating and studying the natal chart, and then later looking at how this will relate to astronomical movements, transits and progressions, pertaining to that year. At the same time the astrologer will carefully balance all this data with knowledge of the client's background, environment, and state of health, to come to some realistic conclusions about the future.

'Newspaper forecasting, on the other hand, is run off in a matter of a few minutes, furnishing the entire population with so-called predictions in the space of just one or two brief columns. Obviously in this process something has to go. In fact everything goes, except for that one piece of data:

the approximate location of the sun on the birthdays of the readers. This is only possible because the sun returns to roughly the same position on any given day each and every year. So, for example, if you are born anywhere between the 24th August and 23rd September the pop astrologer knows, regardless of your age, that your sun was somewhere within the sign of Virgo at birth. He can then look at approximate daily movements of moon and sun and relate these to the general thirty-degree area of the zodiac that corresponds to Virgo. If extraordinarily conscientious, a check may also be made on the daily movements of the planet Mercury, which rules the sign Virgo and corresponds closely to it.

'These form the basis of any so-called predictions. All the other factors normally pertaining to individual birth charts, which vary not only from year to year but from day to day, hour to hour and minute to minute, are totally ignored.

'So, yes there is just that little bit of common language between pop astrology and the real thing. But to criticise real astrology because of the vagaries of journalism and TV programmes is like judging the entire medical profession on the efficacy of grandma's medicine cupboard. A little unfair, I think.'

Note: at this point you should also make it clear that genuine, quality astrology does not concern itself exclusively with prediction. Natal astrology, that is interpretation of the birth chart in terms of character and self-expression, often comprises the bulk of the astrologer's work. You can even stress that some consultants occupy themselves exclusively with character analysis and counselling, and refuse to have anything to do with forecasting. They advocate that character itself will always shape the future, and that when a strong individual will is involved, hard-and-fast predictions are meaningless.

If you really want to press home your attack, mention the branches of horary astrology, mundane and electional astrology and also financial astrology. You can confidently refer your opponent to any one of the many excellent introductory books that are mentioned in the reading list at the end of this book.

Critique 2: Twins

'Everyone knows that twins, especially identical twins born within a few minutes of each other, share many characteristics. These, however, are genetic in origin. If astrology were true, all babies, regardless of parentage, born in the same hospital or nursing home within a few minutes of each other would be almost identical. This is clearly not so.'

Combat: 'Sorry to disappoint you, but it is so, or at least sometimes. We call such babies, born at the same time in roughly the same place, time twins. And there have been numerous well documented cases throughout the world, and throughout history, of such people and the remarkable similarities in their lives. Not only do time twins often look alike, but sometimes, unknown to each other, lead lives of remarkable similarity. Examples exist of time twins who marry in the same year, have the same number of children, and even experience accidents and injury at similar times. Often the family backgrounds of these children are the same, too, the number of brothers and sisters, the father's occupation, and so on.[1]

'Actually, time twins probably lead lives of such similarity precisely because they are not aware of each other. Real twins who live and grow together naturally tend to diverge at times. After all, no one, not even the most devoted of identical twins, wants to be a carbon copy of somebody else. That's why the most startling stories of time twins are of the ones who know nothing of each other's existence, until that is some quirk of fate brings them together. Then the media catch hold of the story and it makes the headlines for a while.

'Probably most of us who were born in a big city have a time twin somewhere, though of course we rarely meet them; unfortunately, other than some partly discredited work during the sixties and seventies, there has been little consistent research into this subject.[2] This is probably because the initial premiss of the investigation would be the obvious acceptance of astrology. Few scientists are willing to stake their reputation on such a controversial idea.'

Note: having said this, it is only fair to point out that not every case of identical births produces time twins with matching characters and life stories. Your opponent may well suspect as much and interrupt you at some stage with something like this:

Interruption: 'Surely you don't mean to say that every child born at the same time and place as another will have identical life stories?'

Counterattack: 'No. Indeed really striking cases of time twins tend to be the exception rather than the rule. Astrologers aren't disturbed by this, however, since it demonstrates both the environmental factor and the use of self-determination in the lives of the individuals concerned, something any professional astrologer worth his or her salt welcomes and encourages. All this is to be expected in the real world with all its diversity and range of opportunities.

'And of course genetics, too, has an enormous part to play. One individual may be blessed with genes which make a particular course of action more likely, aggression, for example, leading to more self-assertion. The time twin may possess a milder genetic make up and therefore not make the same radical choices in life. Some environmental differences can also be quite overwhelming: the material

99

wealth of the parents, the type of schooling, and so on; all these can produce changes that make the time twins' lives dramatically different.'

Note: numerous famous and quite stunning examples of time twins are available. One of the most entertaining is the oft-quoted, though admittedly unconfirmed story of King George III of England and Samuel Hemming. Hemming was a commoner in eighteenth-century England, but shared the same time and date of birth as the king. Hemming took over his father's business as ironmonger on the same day George succeeded to the throne. Both Hemming and George were married on the same day, and ultimately each had the same number of children of the same sex. Accidents and illness occurred on similar dates, and they both died on the same day from similar causes.

Among the more recent documented examples, is the motion picture industry's search for a double to Rudolph Valentino after his death. One of the most convincing candidates turned out to have been born in the same area and on the same day as Valentino.[3]

Another report concerns two American girls who met at the age of six, when their families moved next door to each other. Although unrelated, they looked and behaved like identical twins, and teachers and parents alike had difficulty distinguishing between the two. The girls each had the same number of brothers and sisters; in fact the two families shared almost identical physical likeness, not only between the girls and the two sets of parents, but also between the brothers and the sisters! Both fathers worked in the same place at similar jobs. Later research revealed that the two girls had been born within five minutes of each other at the same nursing home.[4]

In another example, an astrologer tells of how he once encountered his 'double', a man who had the same appearance, same scars, same dental condition, everything. He discovered that the double had lived a life which closely resembled his own in terms of experiences and dates of events; whereas one was an astrologer with antiques as a hobby, the other was an antique fancier with astrology as a hobby. The dates, times, and longitude of birth were the same. They were time twins.[5]

Against all this it has to be said that there are one or two instances of recorded time twins in which the subjects led dramatically different lives and developed highly disparate personalities.[6] Naturally, shared characteristics may be internalised in some cases towards, for example, a common identity of purpose which may not be immediately obvious to the observer in search of external traits. After all, we are all of us much more than the mere slavish fulfilment of our birth charts. The astrological factor will always manifest in different ways; clearly, with time twins, the many occasions where it does so in a physical sense are in no way diminished by the few cases in which it does not.

Critique 3: Earth-centred

'The arrival of the Copernican theory in the sixteenth century totally destroyed the old medieval view of a geocentric universe. From this time on, educated men and women no longer bowed to the old religious and scholastic dogma of the Middle Ages. The mistaken view that the earth and mankind were at the centre of creation became redundant, and the entire metaphysical and theological structure of antiquity collapsed, taking along with it the old superstitions like astrology and magic.

'We now know that the earth is simply a planet, among many, orbiting the sun, itself a star, a mere speck within the galaxy of stars that is itself a mere point of light in the vastness of space. Astrology, in the face of such knowledge, is meaningless.'

Combat: 'Your critique is fairly representative of popular academic opinion, but it also contains a number of common inaccuracies. Firstly, the Copernican hypothesis was not the heliocentric theory as we know it today, nor was it at the time anything new. The earliest known statement against the earth-centred view comes from the Pythagoreans in the fifth century BC. Philolaus, Pythagoras's pupil, certainly considered the idea that the earth, sun and all the planets revolved about a central fire. It is quite likely that Pythagoras himself also believed this and that in one version of the theory the central fire was meant to be the sun itself.[7]

'Much, if not the bulk of the teachings of Pythagoras came directly from the Egyptian and Babylonian scholars with whom he studied during his youth. So the idea that the astronomers of antiquity only ever regarded the earth as immobile and at the centre is certainly wrong. Remember, the Egyptian and Persian sciences were esoteric, never committed to writing. We have no way of knowing for sure if they had a heliocentric view of the cosmos, but it does seem possible. And if so, the idea could be many hundreds of years older than even the Pythagoreans.

'The earliest documented and purely heliocentric theory we know of, however, was that of Aristarchus in the third century BC. Although, like so many other precious volumes of the classical world, Aristarchus's original work has not survived, the theory itself was freely available to Roman scholars in the early centuries of our era, and the concept must certainly have lingered on in the minds of the Arab and European scientists of the Middle Ages, becoming ultimately the inspiration behind the new heliocentric system of the Renaissance to which you refer.

'The reason for the survival and almost universal preference for the geocentric system among medieval scholars was that it was the one preferred by Claudius Ptolemy, who flourished around the second century and is perhaps still the most well-known of the Greek cosmographers. This earth-centred view of the universe was also the only one that could produce reliable ephemerides, or tables of future planetary positions. Because of this manifestly practical reason, the heliocentric option remained largely of academic interest only and became more and more neglected. It was not entirely forgotten, however, and the German astrologer and church cardinal, Nicolaus of Cusa, who flourished a century before Copernicus, favoured and taught the heliocentric theory among his own followers.

'There were, however, also aesthetic and theological grounds for taking the earth as the centre, deeply profound ones, inspired by the philosophies of the Neo-Platonists and, therefore, of Pythagoras and the ancient world itself.

'This consisted of a mystical relationship between mankind and the cosmos, in which enlightenment and wisdom were gained through prayer, meditation or magical ritual. It was the ascent of the spirit or soul, up from the earthly elements, through each of the planetary spheres to the *primum mobile* and the realm of the Unmoved Mover. Much of this was metaphoric, and was recognised and accepted as such by the Church. It was seen as one of the many possible experiences of union with God in Christian Neo-Platonism: unity of the individual with the Infinite, similar to the search for Samadhi achieved through the practice of yoga.

'But, as already mentioned, the most persuasive force in favour of the geocentric option remained that of a simple, irrefutable practicality. Even with the increasingly sophisticated observations of the Middle Ages, the geocentric-based equations still managed to account adequately for planetary motion, including retrogradation, which is when the planets appear to backtrack across the sky for certain periods. The mathematicians had always managed to make adjustments for this phenomenon through the use of what are called epicycles. An epicycle is the circular motion of, say, a planet about a central point that is itself in orbit around another body, say the earth: a complex system of wheels within wheels, in other words. By the thirteenth century there were no less than sixty or so of these hypothetical epicycles in use. Obviously there was constant experimentation with alternative systems and models; it is quite reasonable to suppose that heliocentricity was among these, especially in the light of the links between classical Greece and the Arab world where most of the technical advances were made up until the Renaissance.

'The geocentric system was favoured because it was the only one which worked, but its absurdity must have been apparent to all educated men. The learned thirteenth-century King of Leon and Castile, Alphonso X, responsible for the most accurate ephemerides of the Middle Ages, is reported to have joked that had he been around at the time of the creation, he could have handed out some useful advice, perhaps concerning a less complex layout for the solar system. Yet he knew as well as anyone that to abandon the geocentric tradition at that stage would have been impractical, unnecessary and futile.

'With the European Renaissance came the rediscovery of classical ideas and theories, and, as I have mentioned, men such as Nicolaus of Cusa considered a sun-centred system very early on. However, it is the later name of Copernicus which is most often associated with the new outlook. Himself an enthusiast of Pythagorean teaching, Copernicus published his own version of a heliocentric model for the solar system in 1543. Yet this was at the time hardly the startling, revolutionary tract that historians have subsequently urged us to believe. Its contents even had papal approval! This was a far cry from the tribulations suffered by Galileo less than a century later. Nor were astrologers at all piqued by the new theory. For one thing, it furnished them with far more accurate tables of planetary motion. It was certainly never considered a threat. We know, for example, that during his student days, Nostradamus publicly defended both astrology and the work of Copernicus. Moreover, the Copernican theory still required epicycles to account for certain irregularities, and the real breakthrough came only much later, in the seventeenth century with the work of Johannes Kepler.

'Kepler abandoned the idea of circular orbits for the planets and plumped for ellipses instead. At a stroke, the vastly complex epicycle systems were demolished, and a purely heliocentric model which actually worked was finally reinstated. Again, this development produced more reliable ephemerides upon which astronomers and astrologers alike could base their work, while at the same time opening the way for a total rebirth of Pythagorean metaphysics and astronomical mysticism.

'Kepler, an astrologer himself, was at the forefront of this development. For Kepler, a highly religious man as well as a Pythagorean scholar, the central fire of the sun now became synonymous with God the Father. He was able to discover remarkably close correlations between the distance-ratios of the planetary orbits and the five basic solids of Platonic philosophy, and he developed musical theories, awarding to each planet a range of notes based on the eccentricity of its orbit about the sun, an echo of Pythagoras's music of the spheres.

'None of these highly interesting developments in astronomical theory made the slightest difference to those practising astrology, apart from the welcome increase in accuracy that the new system brought with it. The partial demise of astrology and magic that you mentioned took place only gradually and then not to any significant degree until a century or so later, around the time of Newton. Reasons for this decline were many and complex, and owed as much to the rise of commercial maritime power in the seventeenth century, which used the stars for navigation and trade and therefore for making money, as it did to the theories of Copernicus in the sixteenth.

'Happily, in our own times, modern relativity theory provides us with a true choice in the matter. Here, space, time, and motion are all interchangeable; it is just as legitimate to consider the sun revolving around the earth as it is the other way around. The mathematical concept of reflective symmetry has also always allowed for this reversal if need be, something that was well known in Copernicus's time, incidentally, and even to a certain extent in Ptolemy's.

'Astrology has survived all these fluctuating ideas and

notions. It continues to measure angular relationships of planets to the earth and still draws the earth at the centre of its charts. This is because astrology remains a subject for humankind, for people. We do, after all, live on the earth. In other words each of us is at the centre of our own cosmos.

'Very well — as a scientist or an astronomer — you can tell me that this is all senseless and that we actually live on a speck of dust orbiting around a tiny star lost in the billions of stars that make up our galaxy, which is itself an insignificant grain in the vastness of space. You can tell me that one of the nearest galaxies stands at a distance of more than two million light years, and that a voice from such a place would be just that number of years old and presumably very, very dead by the time it reached us. You can even imply that all the achievements of humanity are nothing more than the blind helpless grovellings of primitive animals on a lump of decaying rock and gas lost in the cold eternity of space and time. While you're about it, tell me just one more thing, where's the sense in that?

'At least astrology deals with life as we know it, or are ever likely to know it, with our environment and our feelings, with our loves and the warm comfort of our common humanity. Copernicus deciding that the earth might, after all, go around the sun didn't suddenly destroy all that, and your suggestion that his work might have somehow rendered astrology meaningless is really untenable unless it happens to be like so many other fables of the historians merely an error that feeds on itself, nourished by simple ignorance and pedantry.

'Ultimately, I suppose, it all depends on your point of view, whether you are at the centre of understanding or merely looking in from the periphery.'

Critique 4: Nations And Peoples

'While one can readily appreciate that an individual life takes place within the larger framework of the State, and that individual birth charts are subservient to national ones, why

106

is there such a shortage of accurate predictions in political or national affairs? If your mundane astrology is a workable reality, how is it that astrologers in this field have no real documented successes? These would surely make the headlines, and prove astrology to all.'

Combat: 'There are, in fact, many documented predictions that have been fulfilled. A fairly recent one, for example, was the nuclear catastrophe at Chernobyl in 1985, and also the English Channel ferry disaster of 1987.[8] However, it is certainly true to say that astrologers working in this field have not always had an easy time of it. Throughout history many predictions have been suppressed by governments who often viewed such pronouncements as bad propaganda. This was as true in twentieth-century Germany under the Third Reich as it was in antiquity under the emperors of Rome.

'Of those predictions that have survived, the most famous to come down to us are those of Nostradamus, the sixteenth-century mystic and astrologer. Included in his rather cryptic works are allusions to most of the great conflicts and political figures of his era, and much of Nostradamus's work is still thought to bear directly on events of our own times.[9]

'In his day, Nostradamus was consulted by many powerful and influential persons, Henry II of France and Catherine de Medici, for example, and it is this commissioned use of mundane astrology that is still much in evidence today. Many of the most powerful and influential men and women in the world, particularly in the American continent, Japan and the Middle East, take on board the counselling of astrologers as part of their overall world view. It provides them with a totally independent, alternative strategy, as distinct from orthodox informed analysis, and thus enables them to stay one step ahead of most developments. Naturally, much of this work is, by its nature, confidential and unpublished, but as recent 'revelations' in America seem to indicate, astrology of this kind might well extend right on up to the Whitehouse itself.

'It's not all hush-hush, though. In our own times there has been considerable open research into the subject of political and economic astrology, including published data, periodicals, and so on. These are readily available and deal capably, in so far as is possible for such a complex subject, with trends and developments in political and economic affairs. If you are looking for spectacular predictions of wars, assassinations and tragedies, you may be disappointed. Modern astrologers do not deal in crystal gazing, and although certain significators are almost always present in the charts of sudden and dramatic world events, such as an assassination, the converse is by no means always true. The charts of nations often produce quite violent features from time to time that correlate to nothing at all in real terms.

'Although essentially superior to individual birth charts, national charts lend themselves far less willingly to the already difficult business of prediction. This is because each human individual has only one possible chart: the one recorded for his or her birth time. Nations, on the other hand, often have several valid charts. Britain, for example, has at least three, including the chart for the coronation of William the Conqueror in 1066, and that for the birth of the United Kingdom in 1801. At least in these cases the birth times were well documented. For if the charts of individual people can often suffer from disputed birth times, how much more so is this the case with National ones! It is far from easy to determine just exactly when a nation begins and what events actually constitute that beginning. Is it the signing of a document, or the moment of surrender on a battle field? Is it the storming of a palace or parliament, or the speech of a great prophet or leader? The answer can be yes to any one of these, and more. Records of such moments are often incomplete, or tend to present several alternatives, as in the case of the USA Declaration of Independence which also has several possible birth times.

'Moreover, the birth charts for the leaders of each nation are often paramount and far outweigh the considerations of the national map. National events often show up clearly in the charts of the Royal Family, for example, or of the Prime Minister, or President, while charts cast for the taking of office, inaugurations, or the official results of an election, can also prove significant depending on how closely these relate to the welfare of the nation in question.

'It might also be fair to say that certain planetary configurations could be so potent in their own right at certain localities as to override totally individual considerations and individual charts, be it of people or of nations. Don't forget, the words catastrophe and disaster each have their root in the latin 'astra' meaning star, and observations of such configurations were actually the backbone of political and economic astrology in antiquity.

'So you see, mundane astrology is a complex business: sadly, perhaps the most nebulous and ill-defined part of the whole subject. That's why it is, to be frank, totally unrealistic to expect astrologers to measure up to some kind of biblical standard of prophesy in this or indeed in any other field. Though, having said this, if you care to investigate current work, particularly that of astrological correlations to cycles in the world economy, I think you may well be favourably impressed by the accuracy of some of the more conservative and sober predictions. Notable in recent times are those of Daniel Pallant, an investment analyst specialising in astrology who occasionally writes for the financial press. His forecast of January 1987, of an FTSE Index level of 2216 by 11th May from its then level of 1675 was indeed fulfilled, in fact just a few days later than predicted, on 19th May. Perhaps only those familiar with the capriciousness of world stock markets will appreciate just how exceptionally accurate this prediction was. The Wall Street market also has its astrological pundits, notably Sam Crawford, who was ranked amongst the top five market forecasters of 1986 by *Times Digest*. And yes, the stock market crash of '87 was foreseen, the most accurate in timing being apparently that of the German/Swiss astro-economist Wolfgang Angermeyer.'[10]

Note: at this point you can perhaps recommend to your opponent the numerous journals and periodicals of organisations such as the Astrological Association of Great Britain, and the equivalent bodies in America, and most European and Commonwealth countries, all generally containing up-to-date articles on this subject. You can find a list of useful addresses on page 215.

It is also important to communicate the genuine difficulties inherent in this branch of the subject. Much of what is expected to be the province of mundane astrology is relevant only to natal work, the winning of an election, an abdication, resignation, and so on. Analysis of charts belonging to individuals is essential for this kind of forecasting, and the problem is that those who are employed on a private basis for this purpose do not, as a rule, publish their findings, while those who are not thus employed must by necessity give only a cursory glance to each element in what is a truly vast field of daily transits, national charts, political institutions and world leaders. It would indeed be a superhuman task to spend even a month of one's life anticipating but a fraction of all the possible permutations of global forecasting. This is why most published work on political affairs consists of 'wise-after-the-event' discussions rather than hard and fast predictions of future events. Also, there is no necessary rule that says every event has to have an astrological correlation. Why should it be incumbent on astrology always to have an answer for everything that happens in the world?

Do try to stress these difficulties to your opponent, who may be expecting miracles from those courageous enough to work in the purely political field.

Critique 5: The Zodiac

'Owing to what is called precession, or the gradual shifting of the spring equinox, none of the signs of the astrologer's zodiac corresponds any more to the constellation that bears its name. For instance, the astrologer's sun sign Aries now falls in the neighbouring constellation of Pisces. With every passing seventy-two years, the astrologers' signs become a further one degree out of phase with the original star patterns. This makes a nonsense of the whole subject, as its basis is completely wrong.

'Even if that were not the case, and the zodiac and the constellations had remained the same since antiquity, it is preposterous to suppose that, simply because a few ancient shepherds, or whatever, fancied they could see the shape of, say, a Ram or a Bull in the stars, that this section of the sky should possess the attributes of that creature and subsequently bestow it upon humans who happen to be born during the month when the sun passes through it. All those stars are at vastly different distances, and not connected in the slightest way. This is the most primitive form of anthropomorphic projection, magical rubbish of the first rank.'

Combat: 'The precession of the equinoxes has been widely known to astronomers and astrology since as early as the third century BC and the observations of Hipparchus. It also seems likely that Egyptian, Aztec, and, most notably, Chinese astrologers, could have known of it many centuries earlier. It appears that some Indian Vedic literature of before 1000 BC alludes to it also.[11]

'Moreover, long before Hipparchus put the notion of precession into writing, the priests and astronomers of the ancient European stone circles must also have been aware of it, since on the mornings of their festivals they would have recorded how at sunrise certain stars tended to set in different places from one generation to the next. These great monuments are now known to have been highly sophisticated observatories as well as places of worship. Not only are they of great antiquity, but their working life spanned many centuries. In short, it would be extremely odd if they, or the builders of the Pyramids, had not observed precession and passed this knowledge down through subsequent generations.

111

'The knowledge of precession, therefore, might even pre-date the zodiac itself.

'The current tropical zodiac with its twelve-fold division first appears in the records around the fifth century BC but its basis was a four-fold division of the ecliptic circle which emerged out of the natural geographical realities: north, south, east and west and the four quarters of heaven which are enshrined in every occult, religious, architectural, and mythological tradition of mankind, from ancient China to Stonehenge, from the Aztec and Greek temples to the Gothic cathedrals of Europe. This is precisely why in each quarter of our tropical zodiac you will find firstly one Cardinal sign, which begins directly on the solstice or equinox, followed by one Fixed sign which marks the middle of the quarter and consequently of the season, and finally, at the close, one Mutable sign that leads up to the next quarter, marking, therefore, a time of change when each season gives way to a new.

'Yes, the conventional zodiac does now begin in a different place. This is because almost all zodiacs are and always have been fundamentally sun-based and only incidentally projected onto the background of stars when necessary. These naturally change with time, but the seasons have always been present, vital in their regularity to all the affairs of mankind and the natural world. Constellations and individual stars have only ever been noted in so far as they provided markers for these all-important phenomena, as, for example in *The Works and Days*, the agricultural poem and calendar of Hesiod in the eighth century BC.

'Therefore while acutely aware of the distinction, almost all astrologers from the time of Ptolemy in the 2nd century AD have chosen to employ the zodiac based on the moving equinoctial points, the tropical zodiac, as it is called, rather than on the constellations. There is constant experimentation, however, on the part of astrologers to determine whether the so-called fixed stars have any value or not. The astrologers who advocate the use of star groups as a basis of the zodiac are called siderealists. There are a few of these in the West, and the sidereal system, or a variation of it, is still in use in Indian astrology.

'The sidereal zodiac has many disadvantages, however, which render it unworkable for most modern astrologers. Firstly, not really too serious, but still worth mentioning, is that the stars themselves are not truly fixed at all but have a slow drift of their own in the sky: proper motion, as it is termed. The star Aldebaran in the constellation of Taurus, for example, has shifted over one minute of arc since Roman times, and this is by no means the fastest. Proper motion of as much as ten seconds per year has been detected.

'Secondly, the boundaries of the constellations themselves are irregular and do not permit the exact harmonic division of the circle that constitutes the modern zodiac and which was probably also the basis of the original zodiac of the Babylonians and Greeks.[12] And thirdly, the sidereal zodiac greatly reduces in importance the most essential feature of astrology itself, namely the basic earth–sun relationship and the four cardinal points of the compass.

'The twelve precise divisions of the astrologer's zodiac are therefore exclusively a product of the inclination of the earth's equator to the plane of the ecliptic and the four seasons which arise as a consequence. If this frame of reference does shift with time in relation to the background of stars, it really doesn't matter. Astrologers continue to apply the old constellation names like Aries, Taurus, etc., to the zodiac signs simply as a mnemonic device, enabling them to fix the character of each sign clearly, remember it, and communicate it to others.

'The notion, therefore, that astrologers are somehow addicted to ancient and poetic fantasies, the constellations in the skies of classical Greece and Rome, with all their vagueness and irregularity, and upon which the entire credibility of modern astrology depends, is totally erroneous. Constellations are simply not that important, nor have they ever been the distinct, irresistible units that one might commonly suppose. Different cultures invariably use different stars to form different patterns in the sky and there are scarcely any which have been consistently interpreted as bearing the same, common resemblance from culture to culture, era to era. A good example of this is our own northern constellation of Ursa Major whose various sizes, boundaries and titles are legion in historical terms and which still retains numerous images in the West even today: the Plough, the Big Dipper, Charles' Wain, the Great Bear, and so on. Similar if not greater ambiguity surrounds the ancient constellations of the zodiac: each culture invents different mnemonic tags and boundaries that best suit its agricultural, climatic, mythological and religious experiences.

'Indeed, it seems most unlikely that the majority of dull and obscure asterisms along the ecliptic circle were ever seen as fancied resemblances to anything at all. Occasionally, titles were awarded to particularly prominent stars which might later have given their names to areas of sky. The two bright stars which feature in the constellation of Gemini are a good example and would naturally be thought of as brothers or twins. But actual pictorial representation, joining up the dots, is a comparatively modern fashion. Certainly in all the available illustrations of the star groups found in Egyptian and Sumerian monuments there is no attempt to superimpose visual images onto the stars themselves, even when these are clearly listed, or in some cases drawn. An illustration may appear alongside the stars or their names, but never actually upon them.[13]

'The zodiac came first, in other words, the images being merely typical mnemonic devices. Ideas and knowledge were always transferred orally in antiquity. In fact it is perhaps not generally appreciated how widespread this practice was, particularly in the days before the invention of an alphabet and the simple convenience of pen and paper.[14] Remembering complex ideas through visual imagery was essential, and the rich symbolism of the zodiac is entirely consistent with such a tradition.

'Ptolemy in the second century AD states in the introduction to his great catalogue of stars, the *Almagest*, that he has not always kept to the constellation figures of his predecessors any more than they had always kept to theirs. The work of Hipparchus in the second century BC is clearly referred to here, since it was said that he in turn did exactly the same to the old catalogues on which his own were based.[15] Unlike other commentators of the period, such as Manilius, this is the attitude of an astronomer, not a poet or myth-maker, an attitude entirely consistent with our modern preference for a moving tropical zodiac.

'I believe it may be quite wrong, therefore, to imagine the old observers giving the name of, say, a Ram or a Bull to a part of the sky simply because they thought they could see there a picture of such an animal. These mythical, it would also seem from your description rather idle or insomnious ancestors of ours, gazing at the heavens and joining up the dots, have possibly never existed outside of the romantic notions of scholars and historians.

'Such ancient and largely nomadic peoples would, however, have been extremely interested in the passing of the seasons and in navigation, both by land and sea. They would have used individual stars as markers wherever applicable, changing these and their names from generation to generation as circumstances demanded. Pretty pictures were not a priority.

'In fact even if we wanted to, most of us would be hard-pressed indeed to form pictures of any kind in the stars. If you don't believe me, go out yourself, look at the constellation of the Ram and see if you can see a picture there. I can assure you that there is absolutely nothing resembling a Ram among its stars, or indeed any creature for that matter. But unfortunately the quaint theory of an astronomy born of the sleepless musings of primitive people is now enshrined in our history of science, and it seems cannot be questioned. It is fed with arrogance and self-importance, assuming the ancient observers to be fools,

115

which I can assure you they were not, and aggravated by the absence of any real observational knowledge of the night sky by historians themselves.

'To sum up: the old zodiac of fixed stars is little more than a relic, a fossil that, unchanging, is stuck in one particular frame of reference, of little use to anyone except perhaps modern cartographers who still use it to form some of their own constellation boundaries. The entire inflated ideal of massive and grotesque pictures in the stars is based on a total degeneration and vulgarisation of the old mnemonic devices that existed in remarkably complex forms in pre-classical times when much agricultural, navigational and astrological knowledge had to be processed in the mind without notes or sometimes without even diagrams.

'Many centuries later, as techniques of draftsmanship became more and more refined, cosmographers and map makers of the Greek world embellished their works with detailed descriptions and drawings of the creatures and heroes which the poets had elevated to the skies, each painstakingly fitted into the vague, arbitrary arrangements of the stars, until by the time of Manilius in the first century AD we arrive at the absurd situation where Taurus the Bull has to be visualised rising backwards with one foreleg — lame we are told — bent double beneath its foreshortened, truncated body just in order to accommodate the grand illusion that one stage further.[16]

'Similar incredible contortions had to be undergone by the other signs as the drive for pictorial representation grew apace. Ptolemy brought back some sanity when he reminded everyone about precession and restored the moving zodiac. But by then the pictures-in-the-sky idea had taken on a life of its own. Still greater elaborations continued into the Roman and Arab worlds. The trend, the fashion spread unchecked throughout the Dark Ages, even migrating into the astrological systems of other lands such as India and China, who already had their own totally different star names to contend with, and then through to the European

Renaissance and the magnificent star maps of its artists and engravers.

'Hence the Zodiac. Historians are stuck with the idea of picture-makers preceding astronomers, and it seems unlikely that their perspective will ever shift to view things as having happened the other way around.

'Astronomers, meanwhile, seem to be the ones most stuck in the past, adhering to the star patterns and shapes of ancient Greece and Rome, and of men and women who lived and died almost two thousand years ago. And if we can no longer change our constellations to fit the zodiac and the seasons, this is due to the conservatism of astronomical science, rather than any absence of technical understanding among astrologers.

'So you see, there is nothing wrong with our zodiac. It is just as it always has been, a wonderful reflection of our planet's place in the solar system, its relationship with the sun, which, in turn, receives the still greater fields present in our galaxy, and which bear directly on numerous chemical and electromagnetic functions that scientists have discovered in recent times right here on earth, functions which have absolutely nothing to do with an irrelevant and largely non-existent fixed pattern of star shapes or figures.[17]

'The whole pictures-in-the-sky notion is one rightly ignored by most modern astrologers. It is an omission entirely to their credit, and should not in any way be a source of criticism of astrology itself. That criticism, when it comes, is usually based on a little knowledge, but not quite enough. The zodiac and the history of astrology is something which can be explored and discussed at great depth, and I hope here I have been able to give you some idea of the actual scope and complexity of a subject which is by no means as cut-and-dried an affair as many would imagine.'

Critique 6: New Planets

'Astrologers are said to welcome the discovery of the three new planets beyond the orbit of Saturn. What seems strange, though, is that while they can insist that the new planets have definite characteristics that aid in interpretation, they still maintain, in the same breath, that the astrology of antiquity was of an entirely competent standard — even though the charts were incomplete. How can the old astrology have been so fine and venerable without the knowledge of the new planets? How, then, could it work so well? And if it did work so well, why do astrologers today need to take the new planets into account at all? You either need them, or you don't.'

Combat: 'To admonish modern astrologers for using the new planets of Uranus, Neptune and Pluto in their charts, while at the same time retaining the utmost respect for the work and traditions of antiquity, is rather like upbraiding the surgeon for using the latest equipment. For the surgeon, the long and venerable history of medicine remains of unquestionable value, but the work is improved by new methods and instruments and the success rate of medical operations increased. Nor is the proven skill of doctors in the past, say an acupuncturist in ancient China, in any sense diminished for not having access to the lasers, bi-pass machines and X-ray diagnoses of the twentieth century.

'Yes, the new planets are a great help. But the old charts and the old astrologers still had it right, to the best of their ability — which was considerable, and all the more remarkable, perhaps, for having less than the full repertoire of planetary correlations to draw upon.

'Possibly that repertoire is still not complete. Always, astrologers have done the best they can, using the best data available at the time; in this respect nothing has changed.

'There is also a further point worth mentioning, although it will only appeal to you if you are prepared to allow an element of evolution to enter your vision of the human psyche. Some astrologers feel that the discovery of the new planets may have coincided on each occasion with an expansion or change in both the material and psychological background of society itself. For example, Uranus came on

118

the scene in 1781, about the time people began to harness mechanical force and social cohesion as a way of transforming society. This was marked by the Industrial Revolution, as well as the political revolutions in France and America. Neptune's discovery in 1846 seems to have coincided with the breakdown of spirit into intellect that accompanied Darwin, Marx, and scientific reductionism, as well as the natural reaction to this in the Romantic period of philosophy, music, and literature; while Pluto came along in 1930 together with the development of atomic physics, multinational plutocracies, the Wall Street crash, and the awesome forces of power and potential destruction so typical of our own era.

'To some astrologers, though by no means all, none of this is coincidental, because the age in which each planet was discovered seems to reflect the character and ethos surrounding its respective counterpart in classical mythology. This parallelism is persuasive when viewed in terms of human consciousness and social change.

'Uranus and his cruel all-embracing authoritarianism therefore relates quite convincingly to the industrial and revolutionary eighteenth century. Neptune, god of the unconscious depths, adds his ethos in the nineteenth century with Romantic idealism and the great and illusory ego-trip of atheism that at the time swept like a vast tempestuous wave through Western society. And then Pluto, the unforgiving, devastating god of the underworld, so obviously manifest in the atomic, plutocratic age, becomes quite readily the perfect *Zeitgeist* of our own troubled times.

'The new planets suit the modern world admirably. For, you must admit, our post-Newtonian person is a vastly different animal, caught in a vastly different universe to that of antiquity. The discovery of the new bodies is almost a necessity for astrologers who would otherwise be at a distinct disadvantage when trying to penetrate the complex character of the modern psyche.

'So, yes, it is just possible, and worth considering, that

not only did the astrologers of antiquity have no knowledge of Uranus, Neptune and Pluto, but also no need for them either, simply because the vast majority of people they were considering at that time did not respond to the special character and special energy now identified with these bodies. Who knows, with time, there may be more planets yet to be discovered. If and when they come to light, however, you can be certain we will all be ready for the change, and ripe for it too.'

Note: here you are showing astrology in the light of change and development. The impression should be that astrology is not static or fixed, but constantly evolving and, hopefully, improving with time.

There is, however, a further objection to the new planets, which your opponent might spring on you at any time: the breakdown of the mystical number Seven. The attack itself may be something on these lines:

'The discovery of Uranus in 1781, and the subsequent revelations concerning other new major planets, not to mention numerous minor ones, has destroyed the sacred Law of Seven so precious to the old astrologers. Including the sun and the moon, there used to be seven planets known to antiquity, and this fitted nicely into the whole chimera of correspondences: the seven days of the week, seven colours of the rainbow, and so on. Astrology must be rather embarrassed now this number is no longer relevant.'

Combat: 'Of course it's relevant! There are still the seven naked-eye components of the solar system; still the seven planets, just as there are still seven colours in the visible spectrum. The discovery of ultra-violet and infra-red light hasn't rendered the seven colours we still see with our eyes any the less complete or relevant, has it? Ask an artist or a painter if it has. Of course not! And in the same way the new planets beyond Saturn have not changed the uniqueness of the visible solar system.

'The number seven is also far from indespensable within the highly flexible and ever-evolving system of astrology, which regards the numbers three, four and twelve as possessing at least equal significance.'

Note: the critique here is typical of those perpetrated by conventional historians when reviewing the history of astronomy. They do tend to develop these wild and, it seems, almost ineradicable notions about the effects science has had on astrology, without ever once bothering to ask astrologers themselves if these claims are valid. A little amusement blended with ironic indignation may be required to awaken your opponents from their reverie.

Critique 7: Conception

'While one must agree that conception and the bringing together of inherited characteristics is not the entire story regarding the making of an individual, it still seems unlikely that the moment of birth can be of any real importance in terms of character. It is simply the moment the baby emerges from the womb and takes on an independent existence free of the umbilical cord.

'The bulk of scientific experience still favours conception and the fusing of the genetic information of the parents as the true beginning of life. If astrology does have any claim to authenticity, it would need to use this moment, and no other. To refuse to do so highlights the often reckless indifference shown by astrologers to the facts of life.'

Combat: 'Astrologers have, from time to time, endeavoured to find a formula for determining the moment of conception: the Pre-Natal Epoch, as it has been called. They did so not because they favoured conception as the beginning of the individual entity, but because they perceived conception as the beginning of each individual organic life, or the animal existence. This was something worthy of investigation in its own right.

'However, most astrologers have also shared in the conviction, common to many religious or mystical people, that the human being is something more than a mere animal. The stuff of life is seen as something external as well as something generated within the organic human entity. Life is part of the ambience, and makes its impress on us particularly at birth.

'The celebrated psychoanalyst C.G. Jung, perhaps one of the greatest independent minds of the twentieth century, summed up this idea perfectly when he wrote that the psyche, or unconscious, is something in which the ego is contained, rather than the other way round, as is commonly supposed. He illustrated this nicely by remarking, with characteristic sparkle, that perhaps there are also some unenlightened fish who believe they contain the sea.[18] The pure geneticist is a little like these fish, believing that all individuals contain their own personal lives and consciousness — a singular entity that comes together at the moment of conception, exclusively a product of the genes.

'One thing that all world religions have in common is the basic affirmation of an individual entity that somehow operates independently of the physical body and which, in its own way, is part of a greater whole. Call it the Spirit, the Soul, the Divine Spark, give it whatever name you like, but such an entity is generally agreed to enter the body at the time of birth and to leave it at the time of death. Countless examples from religious scripture, anthropology, art and mythology confirm this as an essential component of our innate mystical identity.

'Now, of course, not all astrologers adhere to this particular mystical approach. Agnostics are by no means rare in this profession. But all agree that the time of birth is of paramount importance in terms of individual character. Projections to and from the birth chart in the form of progressed aspects and transits give us a good idea of how that individual life will unfold and develop in time, in other words, forecasting. This practice has confirmed the importance of the birth moment emphatically over the millennia that astrology has been practised.

'The moment of birth is, as you have said, the start of individuality, the first breath of a unique life. Statistical evidence confirms the existence of a vital planetary relationship between parents and children at this moment; it has been clearly demonstrated that if a particular planet is strongly placed in the chart of either or both the parents, then it is also likely to be significantly present in the charts of their children.[19]

'That is why, regardless of whether it is believed that the soul enters the body at birth or not, the astrologer has rightly always preferred the certainty of a well-recorded birth time to anything else, for unless you are working under modern laboratory conditions, a chart for conception can, for physiological reasons, only be surmised, never verified; these days no one within the serious astrological fraternity pays much attention to the old Pre-Natal Epoch formulae. Astrologers, on the whole, like to put things to the test. Unverifiable data is not accepted blindly and will be abandoned if found to be false.

'As for the science of genetics, this addresses itself to inherited characteristics only, the animal body of the individual. If you agree with me that we are more than just animals, then you must award to the moment of birth, and the subsequent environmental influence of the first few months of life, a place of importance, if not priority, in the formation of each human personality.'

Note: especially if you are dealing with an atheist, you are likely to be interrupted and told quite coldly that we *are* animals. Our entire individuality is a result of our genetic inheritance. Even our so-called moral status is nothing more than a sublimated instinct for the preservation of the species arising from countless millennia of habitual reflex and environmental conditioning; man is a clod of earth: the naked ape syndrome. Indeed you may well be tempted to believe it when listening to such an outpouring.

Do not despair. Cetainly do not be intimidated. There are one or two excellent countermoves at your disposal, the most notable of which includes Sir Fred Hoyle's remarkable research into genetics. Hoyle, not an astrologer, is a prominent astronomer, mathematician and astrophysicist, and his inventive and independent character has led him along many avenues of speculation, including a mathematical investigation into the viability of life evolving from the primordial slime of planet earth. The complexity of genetic material is something not generally appreciated by most of us; the odds against the right stuff being created through the random coupling of atoms and molecules — in fact the odds against even a single protein of the human body being formed by chance and natural selection — are so great, according to Hoyle, as to be utterly and hopelessly impossible, given the present age of the universe, let alone the much younger earth.[20]

Taking an illustration directly from Hoyle himself and his readable book on the subject (see suggested reading list, p. 217), you can counter any interruption at this stage by simply stating that the chances of one simple protein being formed accidentally from random formations of organic molecules — as is supposed to have occurred in the swamps of our planet not too long ago — are about the same as a person, blindfolded, solving the Rubic Cube. If this hypothetical and extremely patient person were to make one random move every second, it would take about 1350 billion years to get it right, or about 300 times the age of the earth. This is, remember, equivalent to forming just *one* of the body's proteins by chance. The cells of the human body employ about 200 000 different types of proteins.

Incidentally, do not be confused by the results of the numerous 'organic soup' experiments which, repeated *ad nauseam* over the years, have claimed to create the basic building blocks of life under laboratory conditions. These experiments, in which an electric spark is passed through a mixture of various chemicals, do eventually produce organic

124

molecules called amino acids. These are still a long way short of protein molecules which consist of complex arrangements of hundreds of amino acids. Although some proteins have been formed in the laboratory, this has been achieved only by outside manipulation. A spontaneous formation has never been observed, nor is it ever likely to be.[21]

So, in other words, the universe, currently estimated to have the ridiculously trivial age of between ten and twenty billion years, is hardly old enough to have got started on the incredibly complex business of forming even the background material for life. Somebody, somewhere has not been getting their sums right: perhaps because to do so would take us to a stage where some kind of creative intelligence might become evident in the cosmos. In this respect, Hoyle has at least been courageous enough to consider such a thing. He has determined that not only organic molecules but also sophisticated biological structures might well be present within the interstellar matter, a kind of obscuring dust in space which was previously thought to be ice crystals or silicates. Life could well pervade the entire cosmos.

When confronted with these rather startling mathematical realities, the standard textbook champions of Darwinian evolution look decidedly quaint by comparison as they rush us recklessly in the space of a few billion years all the way through from basic protein building blocks to the already amazingly complex single-celled creatures that inhabited the early oceans and then ultimately to human beings with the genius and creative intelligence of a Mozart or an Einstein.

In fact this possible restoration of the human race to a position of dignity in the universe has certainly proved traumatic for some, which is why Hoyle's work is not exactly flavour of the month right now among those who would prefer to view their fellow human beings as brutal animals born of a remarkably gratuitous set of cosmic accidents. Perhaps it is time they altered their perspective; although it should not be imagined that such a drastic re-think on the part of the scientific establishment would lead to any great innovation. Far from it. It would simply result in an idea remarkably similar to what the rest of us with all our quaint and primitive whimsicalities may call God.

Critique 8: Fatalism

'Although it is true that man is often the slave of his passions, astrology seems to assume that such passions are directly answerable to the planetary and stellar forces, or at least related to them by a common synchronised pattern. It seems that the astrologer is cleverly hedging bets with this doctrine. If some of the predictions work out, all so well and good and the astrologer is jolly clever. If some of them don't, then free will has entered the picture, and the customer is jolly clever. Either way the astrologer retains credibility.

'This is unacceptable. The idea that even some aspects of the future are already fixed implies that all aspects must be fixed. How can some things be predestined, while others remain open to question? Either the future is knowable or it is not. Free will in modern astrology is therefore nothing more than a sham, a kind of safeguard, firstly against making a wrong prediction, and secondly against appearing dogmatic and unreasonable — and thus concealing the basically dogmatic and unreasonable nature of astrology.'

Combat: 'Your critique is a fair one, but labours under a certain misapprehension concerning the nature of astrological prediction. Let us agree, firstly, that we leave popular astrology out of the discussion and concentrate on the work of the experienced professional, for much of what you say may be true of the former, but certainly not of the latter.

'The day-to-day experiences of a professional astrologer are usually in accordance with those in similar counselling or advisory occupations: doctors, psychologists, teachers, welfare or probation officers, and so on. All of these will tell you that they see people of greatly varying character in the course of their work. Some who pass through their hands will be positive, self-assertive individuals, able to exercise their independence and rule themselves, change themselves or cure themselves of their ills: people so fiercely independent that their schooling, their social group or even their doctor's prognosis, seem quite incidental to the lives they lead. Others, however, are victims of their desires, their own selfish wishes and fears, so much so that their lives are predictable even to the untrained eye. These are the ones at the opposite end of the scale, sad, introverted souls with hardly any vestige of self-confidence or independent volition, people who seem helpless in their struggle against the "cruel world" and the environment which has shaped them so easily.

'These variations are typical of the human condition, even though the social and material background can be the same for those who succeed as for those who fail. Free will is a variable, in other words, not only from one person to the next, but also from one period of a person's life to the next. Its use in modern astrology is not a method of hedging bets, as you put it. It is part of the philosophy of flexibility and common sense with which the astrologer approaches each individual client until a reasonable picture has been formed of the degree of independence at work within the individual personality.

'Ultimately, it is the goal of any counselling astrologer to strengthen this independence, to urge each client to accept the framework of the birth chart and the way it unfolds with time as a means to self-understanding and self-mastery.

'No, events are not mapped out in advance! Nobody would wish for such a thing, least of all the astrologer. Nor does anyone in the field of serious astrology ever 'see' events in the future as in a crystal ball. If the strange and largely unexplained phenomenon of precognition is a fact of life, then it is certainly not one which astrologers normally

127

employ. Rather, the astrologer deals with obvious practicalities, alternatives, potentialities within the psyche. He or she weighs up the evidence, and draws some intelligent conclusions. These alone will form the basis of any forecast and approach to counselling.'

Note: at this stage, a stubborn opponent may introduce an historical twist and remark that, even though what you say sounds fair enough, the modern notion of free will in astrology is still a relatively new feature. Modern astrology, the opponent may insist, is built on a foundation of medieval fatalism. In practice, the interruption may go something like this:

Interruption: 'All this free will business is fair enough, but astrology has changed its tune compared to the old days. The soothsayers and almanac makers of, say, the sixteenth century exuded fatalism, and were laughed at even in their own times by intelligent people. Modern astrology may be safe enough with its new emphasis on freedom, but if the history and foundations of the subject are based on primitive determinism, how can you expect people to take you seriously now, today?'

Counterattack: 'Yes, to be sure, we do still have our fair share of fatalists, and our almanac makers as well. Pick up any newspaper or popular magazine and you'll find them in abundance. But by the same token, the judicious, the thinking professional has also always existed; a clear distinction between serious and pop astrology has always been present in all periods of history. Market forces have, and always will cater for the weak-willed and superstitious, regardless of whether you are promoting astrology or the latest brand of toothpaste.

'Among educated people, however, and throughout history, the notion of free will has always been a built-in fixture of astrology. The fact that this was rarely referred to by name actually indicates the extreme familiarity of the idea to all concerned. Free will in astrology was always a concept assumed or at the very least discussed privately in educated circles. Often it was taken for granted.

'To imagine otherwise would be seriously, and, I must say, rather arrogantly to underestimate the integrity of some of the most outstanding individuals and some of the greatest minds throughout history. You mentioned the sixteenth century. Astrology was popular then, yet it still possessed many levels of sophistication. Invariably it was a vital ingredient in the mental and spiritual make-up of the educated classes: men like Raleigh, for instance, who, in his *History of the World*, insisted that the stars have sway over the bodily weaknesses only. A man with a choleric imbalance, Raleigh suggests, is naturally prone to the faults and excesses of the planet Mars, but the immortal part of each man can be free.[22] These ideas were as much the property of the Renaissance as that of the Greek, Roman and Gothic cultures that preceded it. There is, for example, a similar kind of view in the writings of Thomas Aquinas, who did not dispute the powers of the stars, but believed that they exert an influence on the "lower man" only.[23]

'It is among the Elizabethans though that we can find some of the best illustrations of this principle. You may notice that it is the choleric headstrong characters in the plays of Shakespeare who bluster against what they mistakenly perceive as fatalism in the lives and institutions of those around them: as Edmund in *King Lear* for example. These are always the villains, the fools of the drama who have to learn the lessons of humility, of modesty, proportion, realism and virtue. The Elizabethan stage bristles with such characters. Yet perversely it is precisely the immature ravings of many of Shakespeare's villains, the hubris, egoism and overbearing pride of his tyrants, that are cited today by otherwise quite perceptive commentators as indications of the playwright's supposedly anti-astrological stance.

'Nothing could be farther from the truth. The informed audiences of the Elizabethan theatre would have understood the imbalance, the weaknesses and excesses of these figures, and would also have recognised in their invective against divination merely the profound imperfections of the characters themselves. Such invective was a device, a dramatic embellishment. Free will was taken for granted as much in those times as any other but it was recognised as an attribute of the wise and virtuous rather than the mere posture of the headstrong and vainglorious.

'"Lear was a man who hath ever but slenderly known himself," says Regan, in Shakespeare's masterpiece. The vanity and unrealistic defiance of those who cannot understand or rule themselves or their pride can only end in misfortune — in real life as much as in the stories and dramas of antiquity. Such was the often obvious moral present in the old dramatic characters which we now miss or else totally misinterpret.

'Only rarely today, as little as then, do we ever see sober judgement triumphing over greed, modesty and dignity triumphing over self-worship and cynicism. In that respect nothing much has changed. Just as always, the world is full of Edmunds, Ceasars, and Macbeths: everywhere from the hysterical financial markets of the big cities to the famine-stricken battle zones of the developing countries. Astrology is far from a cure for such universal ills, but it does help to draw back the veil a little. The rest is up to you and to me, to all of us, and the free will that we each possess, if only we are sensible enough to accommodate it within the laws of nature.'

Critique 9: Forced Births

'With the advance in modern obstetrics and the trend towards induced births, surely there must now be many more babies born during social hours rather than, say, at night. This must mean a lot more people being born with the sun above the horizon than was the case in the old days. If astrology and things like the position of the sun have any bearing on character, doesn't this trend somehow narrow the range of individual self-expression, one child to the next? And, more importantly, if astrology maintains subtle and special relationships as being discernible in the comparison of individual charts, say mother to daughter, then surely induced births interfere with the natural alignment of such factors?

'Taken one step further, if induced births invalidate the natural flow of things so much, how is it that we and our children are still, on balance, a fairly healthy and diverse lot? No one seems any the worse for the new trends. Isn't this all just one more nail in the coffin of astrology and the importance it constantly assigns to non-essentials?'

Note: although this argument seems to be pitched at a higher level than the corresponding one under sparring, it is fundamentally still the same. It is surprising how often it crops up; surprising, too, the difficulty people find in reconciling induced births with natural astrology — whatever 'natural' astrology is supposed to be. It also seems that many of us are instinctively uneasy about artificial birth practices — and with good reason it would seem in the light of the research by Michel Gauquelin.[24]

Combat: 'Yes, it is true that many more births now take place during office hours, almost to order. For example, in England round about the late 1970s it was found that there were almost a quarter fewer births registered on the inconvenient days of Sunday than on normal week or working days, so widespread had manipulation already become by that time. Christmas, too, was shown to be an unpopular time. Fewer births are allowed then, with consequently a sudden escalation in the number directly after Boxing Day.[25]

'As to any possible cloning effect through more births during the daylight hours, this will be negligible. The position of the sun in the chart, which relates to the cycle of the day, of course, is only one factor among many which can differentiate between personality, child to child. As for horoscopic relationships between parent and child, generally it has always been thought that, even in the rare cases where these are not evident in a comparison of the charts, any birth time has always been the *right* time for that individual, regardless of how bizarre the circumstances surrounding birth may have been. Indeed, until only quite recently, astrologers have been settled and content with this position, that is, until the work of the French statistician and psychologist Michel Gauquelin revealed quite clearly that there is an important astrological link between parents and their offspring which is totally destroyed by the practice of induced births.[26]

'During his long and painstaking research, initially studying over fifteen thousand parent–child relationships at a time, or thirty thousand charts in all, Gauquelin discovered that if a particular planet is strongly placed, that is culminating or rising in the chart of a parent, mother or father, then there is a strong chance that it will also feature prominently in the chart of the child. A further survey, covering a massive one hundred thousand births in all, confirmed this relationship beyond doubt. This link appears far more often than chance would allow and is, in statistical jargon, highly significant.

'Interestingly enough, this relationship disappears entirely when cases of induced births are examined. Research is not yet comprehensive enough to know whether or not other astrological factors — cross aspects for example — may compensate whenever Gauquelin's shared-planets feature is absent. Nevertheless, the existing conclusions are clear: that the natural moment of birth is, as Gauquelin puts it, a precious indicator of hereditary temperament.

'This subtle link of heredity and character would be of immense importance in communication and understanding between the child and its parents in later life and would, presumably, aid greatly in the process of ethical and moral education. Its absence may have far reaching social effects of which we are perhaps only just beginning to see evidence, since the fashion for controlled technical deliveries, with all the attendant paraphernalia of machines, surgical tools and pain-killing drugs, has only been prevalent since about the 1960s.'

Note: Gauquelin's findings add a new and unsettling dimension to the recent practice of surrogate motherhood, where an infertile couple contract the pregnancy out, as it were, to another woman. Also relevant, particularly in the United States, would be the sperm bank business, babies to order, where a woman can choose a father for her child via artificial insemination, a father with probably quite excellent genetic credentials but one whom the child itself will never know. One can only shudder at what peculiar astrological concoctions must result from such births, let alone the psychological minefields that are laid for the future life of these helpless adults-to-be.

Undoubtedly, in the light of what we now know of parent–child relationships in astrology, natural childbirth is to be recommended and encouraged as the earliest and perhaps one of the best possible means of ensuring parent–child rapport. The statistical work has been replicated, and there is no longer any serious doubt that such an astrological and hereditary link exists when nature is allowed to take her course.

Yet, having said all this, and despite the findings of Gauquelin, most astrologers still adhere to the conviction that any set of circumstances, and any time of birth, is always the right one: the one that is necessary for the individual concerned. For some, the suspicion that we might be fostering a generation totally out of step with its forebears is taken — admittedly with a certain degree of sadness — to be perhaps a necessary phase of our collective historical development, the mechanical nature of modern birth being simply the means to that end.

Before closing this section there is just one more point worth mentioning. Gauquelin's research can be seen now as a persuasive and cogent factor in terms of the overall credibility of astrology, since it seems unlikely that nature would have organised, no matter how blindly, such a link between families if the planetary bodies had no influence or importance in terms of organic life here on earth.

You can employ this point at any time in your debate as a general confirmation of astrology's validity and practical relevance in daily affairs. But make sure you thoroughly understand the research first. See the reading list at the end of this book (p. 217) for the best way of gaining access to Gauquelin's work, and you will find more about statistical evidence on pages 183–95.

Critique 10: Paganism

'Astrology is a cult, one which has dangerous pretensions towards being a religion. It encourages people to abandon the ways of the true God who has endowed mankind with free will and sent His son Jesus to show us the means and the way of salvation through worship and good works. None of this is aided or encouraged by astrology which seeks to inculcate a sense of fatalism and helplessness in people. It is a primitive pagan belief, based on a pantheon of often cruel and wicked gods who, according to classical sources, commit all sorts of repugnant crimes, from incest to murder, who celebrate their powers by laughing at the misfortunes of the lame or the poor or in stirring up mischief, war and strife, between mortals for their own entertainment and gratification.

'The true Christian virtues of charity, universal love, and humility, are foreign to such gods; their projection through the superstitions of astrology is the work of the Devil, essentially evil and totally incompatible with the lives of decent men and women in any civilised country.'

Note: this may sound a little extreme — and indeed it is. It nevertheless typifies a criticism you might encounter at times, especially if you are teaching astrology locally, or hoping to deliver a talk or series of lectures on the subject. You should bear in mind that although this is not, as such, a successful attack against astrology, to an opponent of this kind it may seem tantamount to one; you will of course want to treat it with respect.

Religions of all kinds are based on many similar, intangible propositions as astrology itself, so you can perhaps sympathise with a person who wishes to discuss and debate ideas of this kind. Our particularly vitriolic opponent here, however, is presumed to be a practising Christian, since of all the great world religions, Christianity at the present time is perhaps the only one to be overtly hostile to astrology.

Many representatives of Christianity, especially those belonging to the more recent Protestant creeds, Quakers, Baptist, and so on, feel that the pagan deities, Jupiter, Saturn, etc., are looked upon by astrologers as in some sense real external beings, and that credence in these can undermine Christian morality if taken in any way seriously. The best way to tackle such an antagonist is to begin by genuinely complimenting Christianity. Show your open-mindedness and your willingness to consider all beliefs: in other words to display the kind of tolerance and sobriety that he or she may be lacking.

Combat: 'Christianity at its best is a highly advanced religion, of course: a monotheism being able to synthesise many disparate and opposing qualities into one Great Being. It brings all the old gods together in one God, and is therefore well suited to the modern mind with its penchant for clarity and economy of ideas.

'Throughout history, however, astrology and its related subjects of mathematics, architecture, agriculture and the calendar, have enjoyed a prominent position in Christianity, not only as outward symbol, but also in the inner workings, sacraments, commissions and politics of the Church itself. Much of this was lost with the Reformation, when astrology was mistakenly associated with witchcraft and magic. It is from this time that the hostility or, at best, grim indifference towards astrology originates.

'The extent of orthodox feeling in those times must never be underestimated; those who even today are only too ready to condemn others as evil would do well to remember the outcome of such righteous indignation. Estimated figures for the number of witch-killings from the fifteenth to seventeenth centuries run to a staggering six million![27] Yet despite this attempted purge of the old ways, all branches of Christianity at the present time still contain, by their essential nature, much that is germane to the sacred mystery of the early Roman Church and therefore, it may surprise you, to astrology as well. To understand this, perhaps we should recall the nature of early Christianity.

'It is now generally assumed that the early Church was founded upon three main elements: firstly Judaism; secondly the story of Christ; and finally Neo-Platonism and the mystery cults of the Near East. All these rich branches of study, devotion and inspiration converged during the first and second centuries AD. They were naturally embodied in the structure of early Roman Christianity, and became in time the foundation of the many diverse Christian creeds we know and recognise today.

'Regarding the first source, Judaism and the sacred history upon which Christianity is founded, we find ample evidence for the use of astrology in the Old Testament era. Indeed, the mysteries residing in the Kabalah are essentially mystical and astrological in nature, and stem directly from the ancient Jewish occult tradition; to somehow imagine that astrology and magic were exclusively the property of the Tower of Babel and foreign to Judaism is a serious error, and one which does not stand up to even the most basic level of historical investigation.

'The second source, the story of Christ, fulfils many of the prophecies of the Old Testament, and also echoes numerous features found there. For example, the story of Jonah and the whale becomes the story of resurrection, and so on. This parallelism has been treated extensively, and forms one of the commonplaces of Christian iconography and biblical scholarship. In addition to this, the historical figure of Jesus seems to have become embellished with many of the attributes of the mythical sun god heroes of the Greeks or the Middle East such as Dionysus, Orpheus or Mithras, whose death and resurrection were bound up inextricably with the seasons and the festivals that marked their passing. Ceremonies such as baptism, and the biblical symbolism of the cave or the cross are also thought to be derived from such sources. Orpheus or Bacchus are to be found hanging from a cross centuries before our own Christ was depicted in this way, while the same number-symbolism and the numerological predominance of Twelve and Four is to be found as much in the New Testament as in the Old — a continuous reference to the zodiac, the four quarters of heaven, and the earlier mystery religions that celebrated astrology. The zoomorphic or animal forms pertaining to the four Evangelists are essentially zodiacal in origin. The evidence for this, found in Gothic and Renaissance architecture throughout Europe is indisputable.[28]

'The third main source of Christian doctrine, the traditional Greek philosophies and the later Neo-Platonism of the Roman scholars, also constituted the mainstream intellectual background of the Roman and Greek world at the time of the foundation and consolidation of the Church around the first and second centuries AD. Ideas such as the Kingdom of Heaven, the Trinity, the Chain of Being from mineral through vegetable, through animal, through man, the angels and ultimately God; the idea of a distinct and indestructible Soul for each person; of Purgatory; of the Unmoved Mover as God: all these are essential to Neo-Platonism or earlier Greek thought and religion. The leading figures of the early Church, Ambrose, Jerome, Augustine,

137

all existed within this framework, this great continuum of ideas. It is impossible to treat the lives of such men in isolation to the vast body of mystical and astrological doctrine common to the classical world at that time. This was modelled on neo-Platonism, and was rooted in the much earlier Phythagoreans, whose ideas, in turn, are directly borrowed from the ancient religions of Egypt and Sumeria.[29]

'Such was the basic chemistry at work in the building of the early Christian Church, although there were of course many additional ingredients. It is known, for example, that the Greeks influenced later Jewish writers, and these writings in turn influenced the teachings of Jesus, making the overall picture a complex one. Yet astrology was one of the few common elements present in each of these varied sources, shared and understood by all.

'Within the Roman world as much as in that of the Greeks or Egyptians, the understanding of the heavens remained of great practical importance: indispensable to the fixing of the calendar both for civil and for devotional purposes. This was the outer manifestation of the deeper, inner cosmic mystery that remained with the Church throughout the Middle Ages and Renaissance, and which can be discovered in the architecture, sculpture and literature of the times.[30] Among the Romanesque style of church architecture, carvings and paintings, we find numerous representations of astrological symbolism: in the Labours of the Months and their parallels with the signs of the zodiac, for example. Pictorial associations of this kind can be traced right back to Byzantine times in mosaic and relief carvings.

'Throughout the subsequent centuries such ideas become endemic to both Church and the lay community alike, both East and West; with time this natural partnership of astrological mysticism and Christianity migrates through into Gothic symbolism, buildings, pavements and carvings. The Roundels in Canterbury Cathedral are a good example. Almost every church and cathedral contains similar items, be it on the grand scale of architectural proportion and stained glass, as at Chartres, or in the humble carvings on village pulpits and fonts. The four Evangelists with their zoomorphic and astrological symbolism, Piscean and Taurean imagery reminding us of the esoteric, solar Christ and the Logos respectively, all these are to be found consistently in places of Christian worship.[31]

'Rather than simply being pagan remnants obstinately holding on to the crevices of Christian iconography, astrological representation in religious art and architecture was a working reality; it even increases with the Renaissance and the Humanist movement in Italy, a movement begun by Petrarch and later developed by Marsilo Ficino under the patronage of the Medicis, and, therefore, of the Church itself. The founders of this movement deliberately set out to blend both paganism and Christianity, adding the ideas of Dante, Cicero, Virgil and Plotinus to the teachings of Christ, to produce a vast coherent system that inspired whole generations of religious thought and artistic genius, men such as Raphael, Michelangelo, Botticelli, and many, many more. All owe their ideas to the Humanists. In the devotional as well as the secular work of these artists, astrological, biblical and Neo-Platonic symbolism are to be found extensively and quite happily side by side.

'On a more practical day-to-day level, astrology was always an essential component of Renaissance court life, to military, civil and ecclesiastical affairs. Popes employed astrologers for advice on just about anything from political or military campaigning, to the most propitious time for a coronation or consistory. In privately commissioned art, astrological cycles featuring the pagan divinities are commonplace in many apartments and chapels; Michelangelo's ceiling frescoes in the Sistine Chapel, and Raphael's decoration of the papal apartments of the Vatican, each combines theological programmes with classical humanist features. None of these was considered to be in the least bit incompatible with a sense of devotion and piety.

'Moreover, the Christian devotion of such astrologically committed families as the Medicis is obvious and sincere. This can be seen by the way in which, when worldly success came, in whatever form, military or civil, it was to God alone that a votive painting or carving was dedicated, not to pagan gods. For although the planets might indicate the unfolding of events, it was the Great Spirit behind them that ultimately shaped the world and the lives of people.

'Examples of this kind abound at the time of the Church's zenith. Above the tomb of a wealthy fifteenth-century banker, Agostino Chigi, in the church of St Maria del Popolo in Rome, is a cupola, by Raphael, in which the planets are depicted. Over each one there floats an angel while at the summit, as in a Byzantine church, is an image of the Almighty. So God is recognised by all as the ultimate ruler, the Unmoved Mover of the angels, the planets over which they have dominion, and mankind itself.[32]

'In the UK, similar ideas, including the great Chain of Being and the angelic hierarchies pertaining to the planetary spheres, are common to the combined Tudor and Elizabethan era. Christian ideology of those times owed as much to the *Timaeus* of Plato as to the New Testament; there was absolutely no contradiction, no dichotomy in the philosophy of the Church regarding the blending of astrology and Christianity. Astrology's intimate relationship with Christianity even survived the Reformation in England as it did abroad in most Catholic lands.

'The later rejection of astrology came mainly from secular quarters, and not from within the Protestant Church. If any debate did arise among churchmen concerning astrology, it was always of the kind to be found in Augustine and, later, Aquinas; this centres on the nature of free will, discussions that are still going on today among astrologers and theologians alike.

'Never, at any time, were the planets seen as living devotional figures or pagan deities to be worshipped in place of the Holy Trinity. As Jung has pointed out, astrology represented the summation of the psychological knowledge of antiquity.[33] The planets were regarded each as a separate psychic force, each a representational component of human nature set within the dynamic cosmic order of God.

'The actual breakdown of the peaceful coexistence between Christianity and astrology came as late as the sixteenth and seventeenth centuries with the Counter-Reformation, the rise of Puritanism, the witch hunts and the slightly more positive spirit of the Enlightenment. Then as much as now it was thought prudent to negate much of the ritual and adornment, the magical connotations of the old Church and, along with this, much of the fatalistic doctrine of Catholicism and early Protestantism in favour of individual integrity and independence of worship. In this climate, astrology naturally became associated with medieval repression and gloom even more than it had been with the Tower of Babel. The current unrest felt by Christians of all denominations towards astrology therefore owes its origins as much to the rising merchant classes of the seventeenth century, with their increased material and secular power, as it does to any illusory pagan or heathen genealogy.'

Note: the argument so far may be sufficient to satisfy those of the Catholic denomination, and possibly even a moderate Protestant. If you are faced with a fundamentalist, you may not fare so well. You have already made a rather disturbing observation here, implying that when a religion rejects its ceremony and much of its mysticism, as has recently happened in Christianity, then obviously something as integral as astrology will tend to share the same fate until, perhaps, a new cycle of fresh paganism starts up the whole process once again.

This subtle presence of mysticism, almost waiting in the wings of its reunion with religious culture in the West, is perhaps another reason for the unease and even horror with which astrology may be viewed. Ultimately, in this case, reason or temperance on your part will be to no avail, and you will simply have to agree to disagree with your opponent. Remain confident, calm and detached, the most impressive defence of all in this kind of situation.

Critique 11: Influence

'In ancient times, the planets and stars were thought to be important because they were associated with the gods who dwelt supposedly in the heavens. The vast distances of the planets and stars were not then understood, and it was natural to infer that they were connected in some sense with the world below. Now we can calculate and comprehend astronomical distances, and realise how infinitesimally small are the gravitational and other effects exerted on the earth by the far off planets, and even more remote stars. There is no longer any logical or rational foundation whatsoever for assuming the existence of any kind of influence from astronomical bodies. In short, the basic astrological tenet that the affairs of people are affected by extraterrestrial forces is not only scientifically groundless, but also wholly preposterous.

'It is perhaps comforting for certain people to believe that their destinies are in some sense predetermined by mysterious astral forces beyond their control but in truth we must all face up to the fact that such forces are non-existent. Our lives and our futures lie with ourselves alone, and not in the minute flickerings of distant starlight.'

Combat: 'Putting astrology to one side just for a moment, you seem to be painfully unaware of the vast amount of scientific research and concrete evidence supporting the existence of numerous fields and forces of cosmic origin which, despite their subtlety, have been demonstrated to have influence and effects right here on earth upon the very biological processes of living things, including ourselves.

'You also seem to think that distances are the only criteria for judging or supposing influence to exist. This, typified by the inverse square law, may well be true for gravitation but even this is open to question when dealing with fundamental biological principles and the microscopic world upon which all life depends. Here, in fact, distance is not especially significant.

'If you like, I can go over some of these recent developments, just briefly, to give you some idea of the progress and scope of current experimentation and its results. The best place to start is with the sun. This is by far the most important body in the universe, as far as you and I are concerned. The sun actually loses mass at the rate of four million tons per second, through immense internal atomic processes that are still far from understood. The sun is a complex body of many different fields, waves and emanations. Apart from the obvious ones of heat and light, the most notable of these is the ionised radiation associated with the phenomenon of sunspots.

'For centuries now scientists have been aware of the eleven-year sunspot cycle. This is associated with electromagnetic variations in the earth's upper atmosphere, increasing when the visible number of sunspots increases. All this emanates from what are called solar storms, and a rise in the output of certain types of atomic particles, which, in turn, affects the magnetic field of the earth and the other planets.

'We are now aware of numerous secondary cycles which are dependent on this eleven-year solar cycle. For example, the electrical engineer, John Nelson, has shown that both the weather and the quality of radio transmissions are affected indirectly by these distant storms on the photosphere of the sun, which in turn seem to be affected by the angular relationships of the other bodies in the solar system. Nelson based his work on the traditional astrologer's aspects — angular relationships between the planets — but aspects as viewed from the sun instead of from the earth. So reliable is this network of interaction that Nelson has been able to establish rules that can now predict radio disturbances with stunning accuracy. Although his work has been criticised owing to ambiguity in his system of measurement,[34] NASA had no scruples about adapting his methods for predicting possible levels of radiation during the manned Apollo missions to the moon during the 1960s and '70s.

'Still considering solar activity, research has now demonstrated numerous further direct and indirect connections at the biochemical level, such as changes in the behaviour of blood cells, which can be in turn related to the incidence of heart failure and strokes.[35] Cycles in diseases as diverse as bronchitis and epilepsy seem, again, to be related in part to electrical changes in the earth's atmosphere and therefore to changes in the original solar cycle.[36] Variations in solar radiation of this kind are also associated with what are called extra low frequency waves which have been found to predominate at peaks of industrial or traffic accidents and which have also been demonstrated to be present during periods of increased suicides or depressions.[37]

'Although no direct mechanism has been isolated for just how electromagnetic radiation alters the physiological process, the pineal gland seems to be the most promising candidate for research. This highly important feature of the endocrine system seems to regulate the other glands, various vital hormone secretions, and so ultimately the behaviour and the well being of the individual concerned, controlling everything from sleep and frequency of dreaming, to the production of blood glucose, menstruation, and the sex drive.[38] The amount of melatonin manufactured by the pineal gland, and which in turn is related to illnesses such as malignant melanoma, is also indirectly related to solar activity.[39] The pineal is of importance throughout adulthood, but plays a significantly vital role immediately after birth and during the first few days of life.[40] Additional sources of electromagnetic radiation may also affect the pineal during these critical early days: a period which has always been of special interest to astrologers, forming the basis of much of their forecasting.

144

'Although the exact cause of the solar cycle is still unknown, once you start to consider it and to look at sunspots and their likely origin, you must automatically draw in the moon and the planets themselves. For despite its vastly greater mass compared to the other bodies in the solar system, the sun accounts for only two per cent of the system's angular momentum, the rest resides in the planets. It seems reasonable, then, that this can be transferred to the sun's surface, causing vortices, solar storms, and eventually those important magnetic disturbances in the earth's atmosphere. There are, and have been, many models for such a mechanism, one of which relates perhaps to the movements of Neptune and Jupiter.[41] So here is a clear connection between the motion of the planets and life on earth, via the photosphere of the sun.

'Although it is the moon which has perhaps the most obvious influence, from the ocean tides to the growth of plants, there are many other subtle effects on organic structures that can be traced to this body — on animal and marine life, for instance. There is the well-known experiment in which oysters, when removed from a coastal laboratory to another location inland, quickly adjusted their feeding cycle to fit in with the timetable of tides for their new location, even though miles from the sea and carefully screened in laboratory conditions from all external light sources. The oysters, regardless of their own internal clocks, were responding anew to something associated with the moon's presence, even though the gravitational influence is minute.[42]

'Many creatures' breeding cycles correspond to that of the moon, including homo sapiens, of course. The length of the female menstrual cycle, averaging twenty-nine days, is identical to the synodic period of the moon. There have also been many convincing studies of crime and mental disorder which clearly establish a variation in intensity running directly parallel with the lunar cycle.[43] It is difficult to study long-term effects on human subjects but experiments with trees certainly do show marked fluctuations in electrical potential resulting from such subtle influences as the twenty-four-hour solar rhythm, the twenty-five-hour lunar rhythm, and a lunar cycle related to the phases of the moon, reaching a peak when the full moon passes directly overhead.[44] Whenever experiments on the human bio-electrical field have been practicable, it has also been de-monstrated that the electrical potential between the head and the chest clearly changes with the lunar phase.

'This subtle bio-electrical field that permeates and sur-rounds the bodies of all living things, including you and me, has been the subject of greatly increased research of late, from a handful of studies in the 1960s, to over six thousand published experiments per year at present. What we are talking about here exists — make no mistake about that, and it is open to the smallest disturbances and influences.

'Still considering the moon, the oxygen consumption of plants has been shown to relate to the lunar phases and to the lunar day, while the natural affinity between fluids and the moon is revealed by statistical research on the frequency of excessive haemorrhaging after surgical operations at par-ticular phases of the lunar cycle.[45]

'There are plenty more examples of lunar influence. It is also worth considering that apart from the direct effects, the moon also occasionally blocks off solar radiation to the earth, and is therefore connected with that particular source of influence in a way similar to its interaction with the solar body in producing spring or neap tides. Satellite measure-ments have shown this quite clearly.[47]

'Once you have established these relationships, all kinds of indirect ones become apparent. We are immersed in a vast network of interactions. Nothing, least of all humans, can be viewed in isolation. Modern scientific research thoroughly endorses the existence of subtle life-fields in which all things share. Experiments really too numerous to mention here have isolated such fields in plants, animals, and people, all of which respond to the greater cosmic stimuli of both the solar and galactic systems alike.[48]

146

'If you take the time to study these findings, I think you'll agree that the evidence for this organic life-field, and its receptivity to astronomical phenomena is quite substantial and impressive. However, it is when we look at direct planetary influences that things really start to get interesting. Apart from the regulating effect they have on electromagnetic disturbances on our own planet, experiments have shown that some direct form of electromagnetic radiation from these bodies does reach us on earth and can, moreover, have observable effects, for example in relation to the metals each planet traditionally rules.

'Experiments in which metal salts are mixed and suspended in solutions, and which allow the rates of precipitation of these metals to be recorded and measured onto filter papers, clearly show a correlation to the angular positions of the planets traditionally associated with each metal. For example, suspend silver in a solution containing iron and then wait for a conjunction of the moon and Mars. At the time of conjunction, the silver alters its rate of precipitation. Three quarters of an hour after the conjunction, the precipitation continues as normal. The moon has always been associated with silver, as has Mars with iron. Similar results were obtained with the movements of Saturn and the metal lead.[49]

'These metals occur in the body. Iron, for instance, is an essential ingredient of haemoglobin. We actually "breathe" through an iron compound in our blood. Iron is also an important agent in the synthesis of chemicals by the all-important pineal gland. Copper, ruled by Venus, is also vital to the healthy functioning of the human organism, particularly the female, and particularly during pregnancy. It therefore has a bearing upon the well-being of the newborn infant. This in turn has numerous far-reaching physiological implications, since our bodies consist largely of suspended salts, solutions of organic material and water. Subtle concentrates of these metals tend, moreover, to settle in those parts of the body traditionally linked to the planets themselves. Lead, for example, has always been the metal of Saturn, and Saturn has traditionally always ruled the skeletal frame. We now know thanks to scientific analysis that lead in the human body is, indeed, to be found mostly in the bones.[50]

'The current state of the art in molecular biology and particle physics tells us that the human body and mind are far from the solid structures one might imagine. They are in fact an almost inconceivably vast collection of chemical and genetic intricacies held together by subtle atomic, electrical and magnetic fields. These fields are inseparable from our environment, from the atomic, electrical, and magnetic matrix of everything around us, from the everyday objects here at this moment right up to the sun and planets themselves. Action in one infers reaction in the others — to varying degrees, to be sure — but all are interconnected in the best mystical tradition, something which is well understood by many of the foremost minds in today's scientific world community.[51]

'On a more concrete level, what may well turn out to be direct planetary influences on the mind and body have been detected through statistical research, the most successful of which is the work of the French psychologist Michel Gauquelin. He has located a firm and definite relationship between eminent men and women in various professions and the strength of planets such as Mars and Jupiter in their birth charts.[52]

'This requires some explanation. In astrological terms, a planet is considered strong when, amongst other things, it is either rising or culminating, and also to a lesser extent when setting or crossing the lower meridian. These four areas of the astrologer's circular diurnal chart, corresponding to the Ascendant, MC, Descendant and IC respectively, have been found to be more frequently occupied by certain planets in the charts of eminent professionals than chance would normally allow. For instance, if you take a sample of eminent sportspeople, the planet Mars is found to be statistically more prominent in their charts than in those of a control group of more sedentary men and women. The planet Jupiter shows up strongly in the charts of eminent politicians and executives; the planet Saturn in the charts of scientists and physicians; and the moon in the charts of successful writers and creative people. All this is in tune with the traditional astrological correlations applying to these bodies. The work has been successfully replicated.

'Meanwhile, Gauquelin has extended his work to heredity, examining the charts of parents and children, a survey covering one hundred thousand births. He has discovered that if a particular planet is strong in the chart of a parent, or both parents, then it is statistically more likely to be so in the chart of the child. In other words, if your father had a prominent Saturn in his nativity, it is quite likely that you do as well, and therefore that your children will. Moreover, only in cases of natural childbirth does this planetary relationship exist. If the births are technically manipulated the relationship breaks down.[53]

'There have been further statistical experiments relating to astrology during the past few years, like the pioneering work of the late John Addey, who developed the harmonic approach to modern astrological research and thereby also isolated some interesting features regarding illnesses such as polio.[54] Although the subject has never lent itself at all well to the reductionist approach of statistical analysis, results are, nonetheless, extremely encouraging. The influence that you spoke of does exist, and this has been amply demonstrated. Moreover, the planets are far from being the quiet, passive objects you seem to imagine them to be. Often bodies, such as Jupiter, which emit powerful radio waves, have jumps in their rates of emission which exceed those of the sun. These are also related to storms, but in planetary atmospheres, not solar.[55]

'The magnetosphere of the earth is highly sensitive to variations in radiation from space, solar or otherwise. This earth-field extends at least twenty times the distance of our planet to the sun and becomes therefore one vast receiver of solar, planetary, and galactic emissions. All the planets, and our own moon too, have similar fields, all intermingling. The vast distances you earlier spoke of are now no longer significant in terms of the solar system, an organism whose parts are so closely integrated that it is impossible to realistically think of them as discrete entities at all.

'The work of the Italian chemist, Giorgio Piccardi, is also worth mentioning in this context. Piccardi, was puzzled by the seemingly random variations in chemical reactions that take place during most chemical experiments. Previously, scientists thought these to be due to chance alone. By placing a copper screen over his experiments, which consisted of measuring the rate of precipitation of chemicals from water at body temperature, Piccardi discovered that these variations disappeared. The disturbing agent, he concluded, came from space. Many years research located these sources in the sun, moon, and planets. Equally important, there was also a strong background variation which fluctuated regularly according to the time of year. This was ultimately traced to the movement of the earth within the galactic field itself, a kind of corkscrew motion produced from the earth's annual orbit about the sun combining with the sun's own motion within the galaxy. In the month of March, the earth's movement meets the galactic field head-on, while during September its motion runs counter to the field of force.[56] The relevance of the zodiac to this may be significant, since the tropical zodiac itself is nothing more than a direct function of the earth's orbit about the sun.

'Now, the liquids which Piccardi used in those experiments are technically termed aqueous colloidal systems, and these are ones on which most life processes are based. The reactions are at their most sensitive at temperatures of thirty-four to forty degrees centigrade, in other words that of warm-blooded animals including ourselves. Like the admittedly far more simple experiments of Kollerstrom and his predecessors, these responses are significant in terms of the

150

maintainance of organic life, indicating a definite correlation with external cosmic stimuli. Piccardi himself, though not in any sense an astrologer, was quick to stress this point.

'Yet for all that this is true, and for all the irrefutable scientific evidence that astrology now has at its disposal, it is also a fact that astrologers themselves frequently remain unimpressed by statistical or experimental evidence, mainly owing to the fact that influence, as such, is not a necessary component in the framework of their art. Astrology can get along quite nicely without influence, and always has done. The idea of synchronised events, of correspondences in nature between the macro' and microcosm are sufficient to explain why astrology works. Synchronicity, thus named by Jung, has as its basis the notion that every moment of time has a certain quality which is manifest in any number of possibly quite unrelated phenomena.[57]

'A good example of synchronicity is in popular music. An old number is played on the radio, a song you suddenly remember from years back. You immediately recall lots of other things: where you spent your holidays that summer, the fashions and clothes people were wearing, who was prime minister at the time, what wars were being waged, and so on. Somehow the old record sums up all these totally unrelated things. Not only is it a focus for memories but also it seems to be a product of the entire world as it was at just that particular moment. And indeed how could it be anything else!

'Time stamps its mark on events; one event shares in every other. It is this special quality of time and place which can be related to the movements of natural bodies, be it the migration of birds in winter or the aspects of the moon and Saturn in an astrological chart. These are all pointers, indicators of parallel events, but they don't need to be connected to these events by any direct causal relationship whatsoever. So astrology, being a mathematically accurate record and projection of movements in the sky, becomes an ideal indicator of the *quality* of each moment of time. Once this concept is grasped, not only does astrology make sense but so too does much of life itself. This is perhaps the greatest contribution that astrology has to make to our understanding of nature and human consciousness.

'As far as influence is concerned, yes it does seem to exist but it also functions deep within the framework of synchronised events. A good illustration of this can be found if we return to the research into human and social events here on earth, and electrical disturbances in the atmosphere. You can say that these are actually caused by disturbances in the sun's photosphere but these, in turn, are related to the movements of planets and the angular momentum of all the other bodies in the solar system, including the earth . . . which is where we came in.

'The connections are endless. Cause and effect, as such, is a concept disappearing from both astrology and science. Everything influences everything else, not least of all the observer.[58] Astrology is certainly very much a part of this observational process. If it also deals with real demonstrable influences — as I hope you now realise it does — then, like the eye, it colours and changes that which it observes. Like the eye, it creates a wonderful picture, based on form and reality but with the addition of understanding and meaning. It is this creative dimension, producing order and beauty out of the data of blind chaos, which astrologers prize above all else and is why simplistic talk of cause and effect, influences from a distance, and scientific foundations are, ultimately, of little real concern to those who practise and interpret the world in this way.'

Critique 12: Relevance

'Alright, so I am willing to believe there could be some rational and even scientific basis to astrology. But really, what use is it all? We live in a world of fast-moving, hard-hitting practicalities. People are sharp and cynical: they're no longer concerned with ideas like this. Even orthodox religion has to struggle to be heard. People expect results, tangible proof, and practical application of knowledge.

'Not only this, but to be of any real use at all, astrology would have to impinge so dangerously on individual human rights as to be unworkable. You can't direct people when and where to have children, or when to do this or do that. Everyone needs to make their own decisions, not to live in some sinister theocracy under the dictates of an astrological priesthood. The whole notion is not only fundamentally distasteful but also, in political terms, down right dangerous.

'Even if you were to direct the private lives of individuals like this, the real practical relevance of the exercise would be negligible compared to the vastly stronger external forces of, say, economics, politics, social movements, or global catastrophes. Astrology may be true; it is certainly an attractive and neat theory, elegant and delightful in its own way; but really what use is it to anyone?'

Combat: 'Certainly no astrologer I know would want to be party to any regime which ordered people about or told them how to behave. Astrologers do not wish to become priests, as you put it; they just want to continue helping others and to earn their living doing something both useful and enjoyable. Moreover, there are plenty of practical uses for astrology other than regulating birth times in some sort of futuristic utopian society. Here, for example, are just some of the many practical applications of astrology, in all its many and diverse forms.

'Firstly, a study of astrology is essential for a proper understanding of history. It is impossible to understand the present or speculate on the future without some knowledge of the past. Even if you start from the premiss that astrology is intrinsically worthless, you will at least need to acknowledge the enormous extent to which astrological doctrine has permeated and often directly influenced each and every period of world history up to the Enlightenment. We cannot possibly pretend to understand the Greeks, the Elizabethans — anybody at all — without considering the one continually popular belief system practised at varying levels of sophistication by all classes of society and at all times: astrology. Without it the historian lacks one of the great master keys to truly sympathetic understanding of the minds and feelings of those that have gone before.

'Today astrology is best used for helping individual people to control their own futures through self-understanding and knowledge. Many working psychologists will now avail themselves of astrological analyses on behalf of their clients, especially if family or case histories are not available. The birth chart can tell us much about the character and emotional background of the patient. It is probably about as near anyone will ever get to a map of the psyche. Not that any self-respecting psychologist would base his entire approach on astrology; that would be foolish. But it is one more string to the bow, and increasingly recognised as such by astute practitioners. Astrology can blend easily with most counselling techniques, and therein lies its value for the specialist.[59]

'It is when it comes to serving the community at large, however, that astrology can really come into its own. The branch of astrology dealing with compatibility and relationships, called synastry, has naturally as great a potential for counselling in areas like social work or marriage guidance as it has for private individuals. In the East, many families still consult an astrologer for matrimonial matters, compatibility and timing. In all cases, partners can discover something valuable about the possible unfolding of the other's personality over the years. Many broken homes can be helped to rebuild, and all the suffering associated with separation of children from parents, together with the ultimately damaging effect this has on society, can be greatly ameliorated through a reasonable and a balanced use of the synastry technique.

'Synastry can also extend beyond purely personal relationships into groups and organisations, and has enormous potential in industry, sport, and education. For example, a teacher with access to the birth data of a difficult child would be able to receive valuable information concerning the possible root of the problem — the pupil's problem and maybe the teacher's also in terms of relating to that particular individual. Synastry doesn't need to stop here. It has further use as a clearing house for those wishing to organise working groups, teams, parties, events, and study-projects. It is able to compare any number of different charts, and produce guidelines for group compatibility and timing.

'To return to the individual approach, perhaps the most obvious use of astrology lies in the field of medicine. The two subjects once went hand in hand, and still do in most Eastern branches of healing. In this country alternative local practitioners in many ethnic communities make use of rudimentary astrology, and much of this could be of advantage to orthodox Western doctors in search of an additional dimension of sympathetic understanding, and who are also aware of the evergrowing popular conviction that the whole person and not merely the symptoms need to be treated.[60] Knowing the psychology of each patient is every bit as important as the physiology; here in the West, astrological data is already being applied by those working in the field of acupuncture as a means of confirming diagnoses, as it always has been elsewhere.

'In addition, there are less well-publicised uses of astrology, in particular the use made of economic forecasting and stock market prediction. This is not to be confused with those publicity-seeking expert astrologers who often make their findings and predictions public, and who are invariably wrong. Behind the scenes, many a powerful investor will use astrology together with the usual considerations of fundamental and technical market analysis to plan decisions. The major financial markets of the world are often swayed by totally psychological conditions and moods.

Astrology provides a useful key to understanding these, though its successful use in this field is a highly specialised subject. It is also one which is becoming increasingly difficult as computers take the place of human judgement in the markets.[61]

'The branch of astrology known as horary, the judgement of events and specific questions, has almost unlimited use in day-to-day affairs. Lost or stolen articles can be recovered, the future course of a business or a relationship can be determined. Questions concerning practically any subject at all can be approached by erecting a chart for the moment the question itself is raised or first comes to light. If you think that using astrology to assist in crime detection sounds pie in the sky, let me assure you that horary was used for precisely that in the days before an organised police force existed. Great experience is needed for this kind of work, however, and it is, again, a specialised subject. Eminently practical, horary astrology was perhaps at its height during the fifteenth and sixteenth centuries, but is enjoying something of a revival in recent times and has many well-documented successes to its credit.[62]

'I have hardly mentioned the use of astrology in personal assessment and self-awareness, that is, simple natal astrology, and currently the area in which astrological principles are the most extensively employed. Here it is possible to make a positive contribution to personal well-being and understanding, something, too, which offers an encouraging and valuable bonus for society as a whole.

'A more widespread knowledge of astrology can bring greater tolerance and patience into the everyday world. To comprehend the other person's point of view, to be able to find a key to those moods which can sweep over us all at times: astrology can help everyone develop such sympathies and abilities. It is firstly upon the substantial world that astrology functions, and here that everyone may learn to know themselves, their strengths and weaknesses, their life's purpose and perhaps their previous history as well.

'Through such knowledge, self-mastery and unity, astrology can guide and inspire in a wholly practical way, providing information on periods of life when advance or retreat, confidence or modesty, can best be put to use. Favourable times for action, warnings of impulsive tendencies, unconscious promptings, and possible sources of mental or physical imbalance: all these can be revealed and adjusted through correct astrological analysis. None of this encroaches one bit on individual free will or choice.

'There is hardly an area of life in which astrology cannot be of use. In this, astrology does not seek to rule people or to eliminate mistakes, nor could it possibly ever hope to do so, since mistakes are an essential ingredient of progress and learning. It can, and does, when asked, offer guidance in times of doubt or crises. It can and does, when asked, offer assurance and inspiration in times of progress and stability.

'It can be abused. Any belief-system can become a political tool. Religion is a favourite. With astrology this has rarely been the case, and the more aware the general public becomes of its genuine scope and content, the less likely this kind of scenario becomes. In one form or another it has always existed, and been of use. There is no reason to doubt that this process will continue.'

So ends our reply to our final critique, and so ends also Part II. The relevance of astrology, however, is something we will bear in mind as we continue into Part III. Here we will be looking at just where astrology stands at the present time, its status in the community at large, where it is heading and what all this could mean for you and me.

PART THREE
WHERE IS ASTROLOGY GOING?

CHAPTER 10

THE ARM OF THE LAW, THE HOUNDS OF THE PRESS

It would be wonderful if the profession of astrology could go into the twenty-first century free of ambiguity and the taint of superstition. Yet the same problems that Ptolemy complained of in the second century still bedevil the subject today: the presence of the imposter, the charlatan, the quack astrologer, along with the gullible members of the public who give them credence.

The tragedy facing the respectable astrologer today is the tendency to be tarred with the same brush as the pedlar of horoscopes. This is as true today as in our view of history. An historian will discover how a certain great writer of antiquity disapproved of 'the Chaldeans and their superstitious beliefs' and assume this to be an attack against astrologers. This is because many a Chaldean immigrant in classical times practised number-divination and gave this a veneer of respectability by calling it astrological. The word Chaldean therefore came to be synonymous with astrology and superstition alike. A curious quirk of history, this: a little like saying that because there are nudists living in Scotland that all Scotsmen are nudists. As a consequence of this kind of generalisation, astrology today seems to remain outside the usual trading standards demanded of the rest of the business community, while it is possibly also thought that anybody who dabbles in such a dubious area deserves all that is coming to them if they are cheated or let down.

The legal position of astrology has always been ambiguous if not also occasionally precarious. In a sense, what was true in the days of the witch trials is still true today: the subject tends to be lumped together with magic and the occult. Anyone who has attempted to teach or talk on astrology locally will be painfully aware of this confusion. Advertisements can be banned, lectures or after-dinner speeches scrapped, all by public outcry from Dickensian individuals, who seem to emerge from the woodwork on such occasions and who, by their sheer oddness, make astrologers look quite staid and humdrum by comparison.

This lack of clarity between the sober respectable practice of astrology and the sensational dark aspects of the occult is, however, understandable when we look at the history of astrology in Europe. In the past, often the best astrologers tended to dabble in the occult: in alchemy, the evocation of spirits, necromancy, and so on. A figure who personifies this tendency is the sixteenth-century astrologer and scientist Dr John Dee. Dee was a man of many talents and occupations: a typical Renaissance man who mixed as easily within the worlds of espionage and diplomacy as he did in those of navigation and engineering. His vision and imagination were legendary at the court of Elizabeth I, but his skills, often incomprehensible to the majority of people in those times, aroused accusations of witchcraft. On one occasion, while Dee was out of the country, his house and library — in many ways the forerunner of the British Library, containing many priceless books of antiquity — was burnt to the ground by an angry mob, on the popular assumption that he was a wicked sorcerer and conjuror of spirits. Dee did, however, have a lively interest in occult subjects, and perhaps the unease felt by his contemporaries was real enough.

It is perhaps fruitless to speculate on the reasons why such brilliant individuals occupied themselves to such an extent with magic and what seems to modern people as irrational fixations. I do not believe it is possible to understand so easily the minds of those who have lived so long ago, nor am I wholly convinced that 'irrational' is a fair description of what is clearly the precursor of much of our current day psychology and psychoanalysis. If we tend at times to imbue historical characters with our own thoughts, awarding them our own particular vices, fears, and pomposities, and then judge them according to our own knowledge and standards, it can only take us further not closer to comprehension. As an astrologer or as an enthusiast of the subject, you might not enjoy being confused with magicians and fortunetellers, with ghost-hunters and spiritualists, but, like it or not, it is all part of the legacy left to us by men such as Dee, Cardan, Nostradamus, Ficino, and Crowley, as well as many lesser luminaries, and to the hostility of the Church to much of their work.

This last point is important, for the Church represented the establishment during the medieval period and the Renaissance. It is little wonder that its censure has percolated down to the present day, a censure that has been reflected and enshrined in many of the laws and acts of parliament that have passed since Dee's times, and in the rather quaint terminology these often employ, with mention of itinerant astrologers, rogues and vagabonds, etc.

Although the earlier Witchcraft Act of 1735 was repealed by a less damning Fraudulent Mediums Act in 1951, astrologers at this time were still classed along with crystal gazers and spiritualists. Moreover, the apparently antisocial nature of astrologers' work has even led them to be included in the Vagrancy Acts of 1824 and 1829! Remarkable as it may seem, much of this legislation still holds relevance for astrologers today, although naturally there is no recent history of anyone being tried for witchcraft. (Homeless or itinerant astrologers are, thankfully, also a comparative rarity.)

In the light of this, the whole legal question may seem rather academic. However, astrologers themselves should not under any circumstances be complacent. Any kind of fraudulent practice is against the law, of course. And anyone, astrologer or otherwise, who offers something for sale when unable or unwilling to deliver is in danger of transgressing not only the Fraudulent Mediums Act but also, perhaps more seriously, the Trades Descriptions Act of 1976 and part II of the Supply of Goods and Services Act of 1982, which imposes heavy penalties on anyone who deceives the public by making false claims for their goods or services. Further measures to protect the consumer are currently being considered throughout Europe and will doubtless add still more teeth to an already sound regime.

It is vital, therefore, to understand the essentially open and provisional nature of astrological interpretation. Predictive work must never function in the language of finality and hard-and-fast forecasts. It is certainly always a danger, not only to the astrologer but to the client, to give the impression that one's luck or fortune will suddenly change overnight simply by parting with a little cash and slavishly following the dictates of a written analysis. Yet this is precisely the message many of the more down-market astrologers who advertise in papers and magazines brazenly give to their readers via quotes from customers. 'Since writing to you my life has been transformed dramatically,' says Mrs B. from Manchester. 'I can't believe the change in my luck!' says Mr D. from London SW1.

Special care is always taken by serious astrologers as to what is said and written in the course of their work. The laws of slander and libel apply as much to astrologers as to anyone else. This becomes particularly important when a third party is involved: for example, in the case where a client may have requested a natal analysis of his/her unscrupulous boss, or where a woman has asked for a chart comparison with her unfaithful husband. The dangers of character defamation in such cases are obvious, especially as the astrologer often unwittingly takes the side of the client. A balanced mixture of honesty and diplomacy is essential at all times. Sympathy is laudable but not a duty.

It is hoped that in the future more and more astrologers will be trained professionally and thoroughly by schools which offer internationally recognised qualifications. Indeed, as a good commonsense guide, most astrologers in practice today could certainly do a lot worse than follow the code of ethics as presented by some of these bodies (see Figure 5, p. 50). The Faculty of Astrological Studies, the Mayo School, and their counterparts in other countries, try to instil a sense of moderation in their students, and stress the need for transmitting this through to the public. In fact the pathway towards a professional diploma from these bodies is one which any astrologer, budding or already in practice, would do well to pursue, even if he or she feels this may not be absolutely essential to their career in material terms.

Established in 1948, the Faculty has enormous practical experience in the profession, and the Open Days and seminars which it stages, regularly attract the best speakers in the field. Until recently it also held a professional indemnity insurance cover for its members. This was never called upon, however, and has now been replaced with liability cover only.

Some astrologers, especially full-time professionals will of course have their own insurance cover against legal expenses or liabilities. Some even go so far as to ask their clients to sign a disclaimer prior to undertaking written work. This in effect absolves the astrologer from responsibility should his or her predictions or advice prove damaging to the client. The following is taken from a disclaimer quoted recently by the Faculty in a communication to its subscribing diploma holders:

> I understand you make no claim to any special or occult power . . . I understand that I am not asking you to tell my fortune in any sense, nor do I understand that you attempt or pretend to do so.

Note that the disclaimer from which this was taken was at the time already used by a practising astrologer. If you are in practice and you wish to design your own, you may be wise to seek legal advice on the exact wording and the degree to which it is binding in law — though whether such an approach is really satisfactory is perhaps a matter of taste. It certainly cannot be inspiring for a client. Moreover, a correctly worded analysis should normally obviate the need for such cumbersome documents.

With regard to matters of public reputation, astrologers need to take special care they do not run foul of the media. I am thinking particularly of the kind of 'Sex, Drugs and the Vicar' kind of coverage that is often found in the Sunday papers or the local news bulletins. Journalists are keen on

sniffing out scandal, and the 'occult' has always been a favourite quarry.

This is perhaps the greatest paradox, that despite the media's penchant for sun-sign journalism and even, it should be noted, in giving their newspapers strong-selling names like *The Sun*, *The Star*, *The Mercury*, or *The Globe*, they still retain an inherent dislike for any of those strange people audacious enough to take astrology seriously. This tendency to take away with one hand what is given with the other is, however, wholly typical of the profession; a paper which will gleefully print juicy pin-ups and pro-macho sex surveys on one page will indignantly report a story of prostitution or rape on the next, all without the slightest vestige of unease over their possible hypocrisy.

Television can appear more fair, and may often seem to be informative on subjects like astrology. But then witness preparations in 1975 for the BBC's science review programme *Horizon* and its investigation of astrology. Although the programme itself when screened had the appearance of impartiality, much positive experimental work was excluded from the final presentation. The metal salt experiments of Kollerstrom were filmed, but despite the fact that they showed irrefutable evidence for a planetary effect (or perhaps precisely because they showed irrefutable evidence for a planetary effect) this particular contribution was dropped, and the footage itself destroyed![1] Yes, destroyed. Not even an impartial researcher in the near or distant future will be able to trace this highly interesting experiment in the film archives of the BBC.

On a more encouraging note, both TV and newspapers alike now often feature that slightly more positive and responsible style of investigative journalism that acts as watchdog to the consumer. Although this can often be unpleasantly wary of anyone connected with psychology, the healing or the counselling arts, such monitoring of standards may not be such a bad thing for astrology as a whole. It can weed out the tricksters, the plainly fraudulent

167

and bad astrologers, who are thankfully few in number perhaps precisely because of this kind of journalism. As is so often the case, the freedom of the press turns out to be one of the most valuable assets of any democratic society.

Astrologers in the future need not go in fear, therefore. If they are sincere they will be spared. What they will have to do, though, is foster awareness: a continued familiarity with the real world and the ever-changing climate of public opinion; for it is amazing how little causes most people to feel indignant and hard done by, and to suddenly demand an expose of the culprit. Astrologers need to steer clear of sensitive issues and monitor within themselves any fault or indiscretion that might encourage the attentions of crusading journalists.

Like any profession, astrology will only ever be as good as its practitioners. Again, as has been mentioned so often in these pages, modesty, humility, and a firm reluctance to promise miraculous predictions and revelations, be it to fee-paying clients or to your friends and acquaintances, remain the best defence of all. All this isn't easy of course. There are many obstacles. There are cautionary tales that need to be heeded. Let's look at some of these next.

CHAPTER 11
CAUTIONARY TALES

Since nature has on the whole not been able to make us perfect,
it is only fair that she has at least made us blind to our faults.
Were this the only reason, it would be sufficient for us to be
wary, to step back occasionally and check our own behaviour. As
an enthusiast or practitioner of astrology, you are first and
foremost a guardian of a venerable and precious tradition, and
you must conduct your affairs accordingly — that is, as far as
possible, impeccably.

The Sage keeps the One and becomes the standard for
   the world.
He does not display himself; therefore he shines.
He does not approve himself; therefore he is noted.
He does not praise himself; therefore he has merit.
He does not glory in himself; therefore he excels.
And because he does not compete; therefore no one in
   the world can compete with him.[1]

THE SPECIALIST'S TALE

First of all let's have the story of the astrologer, usually a
highly paid professional, who although an excellent practitioner lacks any real knowledge of the wider implications
of his or her art — the relation of astrology to history, to
psychology, the sciences, and so on. This person is often left
at a disadvantage when confronted by experts in any of

these fields; or might also be too deeply immersed in his or her own ways to be of any real use or assistance to those who come for help or guidance.

Every astrologer needs to remain approachable: not to become walled in by specialisation. This is going to become more and more important during the years ahead, as the world moves further and further into a situation where knowledge has to be compartmentalised and where so many jobs can only be handled by experts. Then, as never before, we will need people who can see the whole picture, contemplate alternatives. An astrologer who can provide this service will always be invaluable to his or her clients in an emotional sense, especially in times of crises when it often seems there is no way out, no way to turn. On the other hand, the narrow, specialist astrologer in this kind of world becomes caught in the same trap as those he or she seeks to advise, and everyone suffers as a consequence.

It is vital, therefore, to keep learning, to read, listen and to study anything and everything that seems in any way relevant to astrology. And most things are relevant. Astrology embraces all of life, from the sacred to the profane.

THE PRIMA DONNA'S TALE

The 'persona' is a term employed by psychology to describe our self-image, the face or mask we all, to a greater or lesser extent, put on each day in order to fulfil our social functions. The traffic warden becomes wholly a traffic warden the moment he or she dons the uniform and takes to the streets, otherwise we might not take them quite so seriously as we do. When challenged we often defend our personas vehemently, as if our lives depend on it. This can result in a genuine neurosis in certain individuals who may identify with the persona to such a degree that they lose touch with the real inner self and its needs.

A great danger for astrologers is that of taking their persona so seriously as to be beyond reach. These distant, formal figures of mystery are not likely to be able to serve the public nor to inspire much trust in even those closest to them. Also, enthusiasts of astrology who, even if ever so sincere, nevertheless appear exceptionally eccentric to the vast majority of people, are not likely to advance their cause, no matter how well informed or erudite. This is perhaps a rather sad state of affairs; for the 'weirdo' astrologer or pseudo-occultist is, once removed from his narrow band of associates and friends, invariably a figure of hilarity, pity or contempt. It is up to each of us to appraise with honesty just how much of this weakness we have within ourselves.

It may seem to many readers that to bring matters of personal appearance into this is to descend into preaching. But we all have to live in the real world, and the demon-

stration of a willingness to meet society, with all its faults and imperfections, at least half-way is a sign which others generally respect and, most important of all, trust.

It might also be worth remembering that genuine character is not created or enhanced by appearance and attitude. If you are an interesting person and have something wonderful like astrology to offer the world, you do not need to look particularly outstanding or eccentric. It is usually the transparently fake mystic, whose main intent is merely to provide themselves with an unusual and attractive veneer of occultism and fascination, who is the first one to advertise the fact by outward appearance. The real thing, however, has no need of display.

THE INVALID'S TALE

Yes, astrologers amateur or professional are only human, prone to 'the thousand natural shocks that flesh is heir to'. Inevitably, when your foot is in plaster, or your car in for body-repairs, when you lose your job or your house, or all together, some smart aleck is going to ask you why you didn't see it coming. The crystal ball will seem to have broken down and, oh dear, how ironic! It becomes a joke as old as the notice outside the fortuneteller's hut on the pier . . . 'Closed Due To Unforeseen Circumstances.'

Yes, it can be embarrassing but, as most astrologers know from bitter experience, when life's little accidents come along they are rarely totally unexpected. It is often the case that you have located a particularly unpleasant period ahead but are unable to pinpoint exactly the field of effect. Something nasty is likely to happen, but what exactly is almost impossible to determine. Locking yourself indoors for six weeks or so while the offending planetary configuration passes, is hardly a practical solution. Hence it often seems as though you have been taken unawares.

Not to worry. There are plenty of ways around it. Firstly, you can try your best to employ a reputable astrologer in the first place, or if you already are a professional, make sure you forecast your own affairs accurately. Of course, if you have a busy schedule this can become something of a chore, so it might be worth the effort to arrange a reciprocal forecast every once in a while with another astrologer, as it is undoubtedly easier to forecast for somebody else than for oneself. Such an arrangement would be of value and interest to both parties.

Failing that, the best solution is, again, to practise that impeccable attitude, in other words humility. An astrologer who does not glory in personal powers during the good times is less likely to be the butt of teasing or ridicule when faced with personal problems and misfortunes during the bad.

Also, there are one or two good replies which can be directed against someone who is being especially vindictive. When they ask why it was you didn't see it coming, simply look them up and down calmly and answer, 'What makes you think I didn't?' A slightly enigmatic attitude here will work wonders. If the adversary is tenacious, however, and insists that, even if you did know, you should have taken steps to prevent it, you will need to explain things a little more fully. Your reply need not be a long soliloquy on the vagaries of fate and free will. Just remind your adversary that to insulate oneself against the bad things in life is also to shut out the good. In other words, the hard times are all part of the package. Simple as that.

THE REBEL'S TALE

A further note of caution has to be sounded in terms of political gullibility and the tendency for astrology to appear 'esoteric' and mildly anti-establishment. It is perhaps natural to expect an astrologer to be conscious of social issues but someone genuinely open-minded will rarely take such interests to an extreme. The extremist, on the other hand, can be drawn to astrology, particularly to natal and mundane astrology, and those who slip into the habit of using this as a ready-made political platform are perhaps the most obvious offenders. It is here that the golden rule of chart interpretation, i.e. that personal preferences and prejudices should never, under any circumstances interfere with judgement, is neglected at our peril.

If you are a customer, it is easy to spot this type, since he or she usually makes the worst kind of astrologer. Their interest in you is likely to be more in your degree of social awareness rather than any personal matter you may wish to discuss. This attitude filters through into their written work as well: an enduring medium by which the profession will normally be judged. Always you will find the same implicit bias against the evils of capitalism or imperialism, always the same smug irony: a kind of camp disenchantment with anything remotely associated with law or authority or the mythical bourgeoisie. Astrology really takes second place for these practitioners, and they should be avoided at all costs.

It is, again, up to each of us to examine the extent to which we allow internal inadequacies to colour politically our astrology, inadequacies such as frustrated vanity, the desire to be known as vaguely anarchic, or to appear a little bit 'dangerous' and a trifle more exciting and interesting than would otherwise be the case. It really is vitally important for us all to be aware of this danger. For if anything is likely to render astrology laughable and batten it down to the lunacies and irrationalities of the past, it would be an

extreme political philosophy which itself may be no more than a grotesque anachronism in the eyes of the vast majority of rational balanced men and women.

THE NAME-DROPPER'S TALE

It is often tempting, when arguing for astrology to bring in names of distinguished individuals who have supported the subject or actually practised it themselves. The list in Part I (see p. 41) provides you with the names of some of these but for reasons of discretion, you will find few contemporary names in there. In any case, unless you are absolutely certain that a particular living person, famous or not, explicitly favours astrology, you should not under any circumstances cite his or her name in debate. You may well be correct in saying that such-and-such a person is pro-astrology but you may also be let down later by a denial from that same individual. This will make you look foolish indeed. Remember, the more prominent a person is the less he or she will wish to have their personal beliefs aired in public, while the professional astrologer should of course never disclose the names of his or her clients to anyone, for any purpose.

Quoting the names of people who share your views is hardly a satisfactory form of argument in any case, and even if you do stick to historical personages, beware of name-dropping too freely. A clever and erudite opponent may be able to respond with quotations by one or two of the names you have mentioned which seem to doubt or even criticise astrology. This is often as much due to semantics as anything else, confusion arising over precisely what the word 'astrology' or 'astronomy' meant to the writer or speaker in question.

To illustrate this point, we can take two quotations from the writings of Johannes Kepler (1571–1630). One of the most important figures in the history of astronomy, and indeed of science, Kepler was also an astrologer. His first publication, *De Fundamentis Astrologiae Certioribus*, of 1602, was entirely in support of the astrological hypothesis. In its genuine state, astrology remained a lifelong interest for Kepler, though conventional scholars are rather distressed by this fact, and often quote from Kepler's works and letters in order to unearth a supposedly anti-astrological stance:

'No one should regard it as impossible that, from the follies and blasphemies of astrologers, may emerge a sound and useful body of knowledge.' Or, still more damning, 'Astrology — the foolish daughter, selling herself to maintain the wise mother of astronomy.'[2]

In order to put these two quotations into perspective it is necessary to remember two important things: firstly, that pop astrology and the casting of cheap horoscopes was as prevalent in Kepler's day as it is in our own, and secondly

that these quotes, in translation, reflect the attitude of the writer to the way he would like to think of Kepler behaving, as the founder of modern astronomy, rather than a man who busied himself with Pythagorean metaphysics. The original German has the adjective 'buhlerische' to describe the daughter, which does not mean foolish at all, but something closer to 'wanton'. In other words, Kepler may have thought of popular astrology as wasteful but certainly not foolish.

Also, we have to realise that for Kepler astronomy was a science vastly different to the subject that goes by that name today. Astronomy, for this highly original and inventive man, was in fact an elevated and refined astrology, a science which could describe the living, mathematical cosmos but which would also reflect the high metaphysical ideals of antiquity. The 'wise mother' in this case was not the astronomy of dry lifeless facts and figures that now confront us in the text books of our universities but was in fact astrology with a scientific mathematical content, a perfect synthesis of the physical and metaphysical worlds.

In other cases, quotations may be thrown back at you from figures such as Augustine or Aquinas. Both these men were at times ambivalent to astrology. They were disturbed by the tendency for astrology to seem fatalistic, especially when practised 'wantonly', as Kepler might have put it, without the natural mystical content of Neo-Platonism and early Christianity. Often, they were required to make statements of an anti-astrological nature for purely diplomatic or doctrinal reasons. Often, too, such men would lose their taste for radical ideas in old age when intellectual quietism had set in.

Be prepared for these inconsistencies, and do not be deterred by them. Human beings are complicated things, and opinions and beliefs often change dramatically within the space of one lifetime. Indeed, such change is a sure indication of an open mind and a developing psyche. Generally it is not advisable, therefore, to stake your case wholly on the sympathetic attitude of any one historical figure. Some of the people in our list will have led foolish and even quite appalling lives. In any case, astrology can provide ample protection and evidence in its own right without needing to draw continually on historical precedents. Certainly these can add weight to any defence but do not rely on them for a shield.

Finally, a word about conventional scholars, especially from the earlier part of this century who have often been bitterly antagonistic towards astrology. An educated opponent may do a little name-dropping of his or her own occasionally; figures such as Neugebauer, Eisler, and so on, may be cited in discussion or correspondence. Unfortunately, some of the best source books on the history of astronomy often contain numerous and heavily laboured comments against what are seen as the superstitions and follies of the past. Persona is at stake here, transparently so, and a kind of nervous, apologetic tone pervades the work whenever astrological references need to be made, the writers having to overstate constantly the fact that they do not give any credence to such tedious details as the zodiac or the mystical origins of astronomy, etc. Often, too, the authors in question have not studied practical astrology sufficiently to be able to pass judgement, and their descriptions of the subject often contain inaccuracies and mistakes.

So, while it is wrong, and certainly not wise to denigrate any work of scholarship, do not be impressed if your opponent quotes from such sources as a means towards criticising astrology. If he or she needs to resort to such secondhand tactics, the argument is obviously flawed, and you should be able to overcome it immediately.

Happily, today, the situation has improved. Even conventional writers on astronomy manage to treat its great ancestor astrology with some of the respect it deserves. For every embittered scholar who has railed against the subject in the past, there are now many who approach it with fairness and equanimity.

THE GURU'S TALE

The would-be astrologer looking for a sensational image is also prey to one other great enemy and opponent that we have not dealt with as yet: the well-meaning but rather naive 'fan' or admirer. Don't be flattered by people who hang on your every word as if it were about to be carved in stone. Being seen to bask in adulation and to feed on the weaknesses of others will not raise your reputation one bit — in fact quite the reverse.

Just do what needs to be done.
Never take advantage of power.
Achieve results,
But do not glory in them.
Achieve results,
But never boast.[3]

There is yet a further danger for the guru astrologer: simply frightening people off. Of course you can decide to specialise on the spiritual level, and maybe your clients or friends will respond to that. You can light the joss sticks and introduce them immediately to your disembodied guide on the astral plane if you like but remember, if you are in professional practice, the average man or woman coming to visit you for the first time is likely to be nervous. They have a right to expect you to behave sensibly and, at least for the time being, reasonably.

So instead of ego-tripping, try always to be understanding, firm, and honest with your clients and your admirers. Impress on them how astrology has to be approached in a spirit of realism and caution, that you are simply an ordinary representative of the art as it stands today and not some kind of prophet or messianic figure of the Aquarian Age.

Are there any more cautionary tales? Probably as many as there are astrologers to tell them. By the nature of the subject you will be functioning in pretty rarefied air, up high, where a fall is always possible. Do not worry. Go ahead and be what you are. Remember that fortune favours the brave.

CHAPTER 12
LIES, DAMNED LIES, AND STATISTICS

In recent years there has been a good deal of activity and research in the area of astrological statistics, something which, for good or bad, seems likely to continue, especially with the ready availability of powerful computers. Everyone interested in astrology should be familiar with at least a smattering of these trends in order to become a true all-round competitor in the art of self-defence.

The statement, often made, that you can prove anything with statistics is perhaps a rather smug and cynical one. Such technical understanding is a great aid and comfort in our search for knowledge and awareness of the world in which we live. There is no reason why astrologers, too, should not employ statistics occasionally to demonstrate their claims or to defend themselves when challenged at that level. However, remember that a good astrologer has no more need of statistics to justify his or her position than has, say, an accomplished artist, a political leader or a good friend. The deeds, the thoughts and the simple integrity of such people are sufficient. Nor do all astrologers necessarily believe statistical research to be useful or even desirable. Opinions differ widely.

In addition to this, a state of warfare now seems to exist between astrologers and certain sections of the scientific community. It is difficult to know who actually first commenced hostilities but some scientists, in the face of astrology's increasing popularity, have felt the need to hit back with statistics of their own, as well as one or two emotional outbursts of quite amazing intemperance and irrationality.

For example, in 1975 it was thought prudent for a group of scientists to publish a kind of public rebuttal of the subject. This took the form of a statement, drafted by astronomer Bart Bok and signed by 186 'leading' scientists, which appeared in the American magazine, *Humanist*. The statement, which was also circulated to many other newspapers and periodicals, urged its readers to consider the evils and perils of astrology and the impossibility of it possessing any rational scientific foundation.[1] The response of astrologers was to publish their own counter-declaration, signed not by 186 but by 187 academically distinguished people who were either astrologers themselves or else believed the subject to present a valid area for investigation and research.[2]

So, a kind of childish tit-for-tat exchange had already emerged, the first statement based, as most people realised, on hysteria and a total lack of empirical evidence or understanding, and the second, although far more reasonable in tone, being almost equally as paranoid. The battle had begun. Astrology had entered the world of modern warfare. The fact that it all seemed to resemble so much hot air, a little like the small boys not being allowed to play with the big boys, was beside the point. Egos were at stake, the persona of the professional threatened. Astrologers and scientists alike began to squirm and squabble as though their sanity depended on sustaining their own particular claims and prejudices.

There is even an organisation in the United States — the Committee for the Scientific Investigation into Claims of the Paranormal — a kind of self-styled police force which regularly takes a swipe at astrology in its own quarterly journal, especially at those times when astrology believes it has some kind of proof to announce to the world.

To date there have been numerous experiments, many attempts at statistical analysis of astrology, both for and against the subject. With few exceptions these have proved hopelessly inadequate. The basic problem until recent times was that astrologers were poor statisticians, while statisticians themselves were weak in their understanding of the subtle mechanisms of astrology.

To illustrate some of these difficulties in real terms, we will look briefly at two recent experiments, one in favour of astrology, the other against.

In the late sixties the distinguished British astrologer, Jeff Mayo, founder of one of the foremost colleges for astrologers and a noted writer on the subject, initiated an experiment on zodiac signs and the way in which each sign's polarity, positive or negative, relates to individual character. To do this a number of people were asked to assess their own personality through a questionnaire which was, in turn, compared with the volunteer's sun sign.[3]

The degrees of extraversion or introversion indicated by these questionnaires were then projected onto the six positive and six negative sun signs of the zodiac, traditionally associated with extraversion and introversion respectively. This subsequently revealed an amazing correlation between the personalities and the signs. Those born under the positive signs of Aries, Gemini, Leo, and so on, returned questionnaires which were on balance plainly extraverted, while the subjects born under the negative signs of Taurus, Cancer, Virgo, and so on, really did come across as the deep, introverted types. All well and good. The problem with this experiment, as it later transpired, was that many of the subjects participating in the research were taken from among Jeff Mayo's own students, who were already familiar with sun sign doctrine and hence the exact level of introversion/extraversion that might be expected of them. And although Jeff Mayo has since undertaken far more sophisticated and encouraging work in this field, his oversight in this case is typical of those committed by researchers early on, when they are not yet familiar with the rigours of statistical analysis. Experiment invalid.

185

In 1985 an experiment, conducted by Shann Carlson of the Department of Physics, Berkely, was published in the scientific journal, *Nature*. Here, Carlson claimed to have disproved astrology conclusively.[4] Indeed, reading the introduction and the concluding remarks of Carlson's article, one would have to admit the author had succeeded admirably in doing just that. Studying the experiment itself, however, left the impartial observer in some doubt. Apparently even a member of the original research team felt she had to resign early owing to an inherent bias in the experiment itself which was almost guaranteed to produce negative results.[5]

A complex experiment, featuring a double-blind test, it began with a group of volunteers who were each asked to complete a questionnaire called a CPI, which is short for California Personality Inventory, and which produces a character profile of a highly specialised kind, intelligible only to trained psychologists. The CPIs, plus two other 'fake' control ones for each volunteer, were then sent with birth data to a number of participating astrologers (who really should have known better) with the requirement that without any personal contact with the volunteers themselves they cast a birth chart for each one and then try to pick out the correct CPIs. In other words could the astrologer match the correct character profile to its owner's horoscope?

At the same time the astrologers were obliged to write character analyses for these charts, based on their own interpretations, and return these to the examiners. The correct one was in turn presented for each volunteer's appraisal, along with two other 'fake' control interpretations. Each volunteer was then required to pick out the one most closely resembling his or her own personality.

Unfortunately, a little earlier, when asked to pick out their own CPIs based on the original personality test, the subjects had great difficulty in recognising their own one — such is the accuracy and relevance of the CPIs themselves without the necessary expert analysis for which they are designed. Because of this difficulty, the second half of the experiment was scrapped. The earlier part, however, the astrologers' contribution, was retained, and results produced showing that they were, statistically, unable to pick out the correct CPIs from the controls any more than chance would normally allow.

How the poor astrologers were supposed to select the correct CPIs when even the people to whom they belonged were unable to do so is puzzling, nevertheless, this was cited as conclusive proof that the astrological hypothesis had been refuted.

A further slant to the experiment was that the sex of each volunteer was not included in the data presented to the astrologers, yet this is one of the most vital pieces of information needed, not only for any worthwhile astrological analysis, but also for the correct interpretation of the CPI! This, note, is the work of a respected scientist.

Fortunately, human character is rather more complex and intricate than the mere delineation and outcome of personality tests, which is not surprising to anyone who has studied human nature but which might come as a shock to others engaged in more specialised fields. Experiment invalid.

Statistics can be used intelligently however, and when they are they constitute an important part of the modern armament, for both astrologer and — sadly — cynics alike. It is necessary therefore to be aware of the successes in this field, particularly the work of the French statistician and psychologist Michel Gauquelin (pronounced rather like Cork-a-lan). A small book of this nature can hardly do justice to the work of this dedicated and tenacious man but we should at least be able to draw our opponent's attention to the basic results of his work if we are ever challenged from a purely technical or scientific standpoint. As you might already have noticed, I have cited Gauquelin's research frequently in Part II. It deserves to be mentioned here as well, however, and needs to be looked at in more detail.

Over the years, Gauquelin has studied many thousands of charts, and has submitted them to rigorous and exhaustive statistical analysis. In this he has been particularly successful in isolating a high frequency of strong planetary placements in the charts of eminent professionals such as athletes, doctors, actors, and so on. In this context, a planet is considered strong when it is rising, setting or crossing the upper or lower meridian of the birth chart. Gauquelin's results are remarkable. For instance, the traditionally energetic and aggressive planet Mars is shown quite conclusively to be more frequently strong in the charts of sportsmen than chance would normally allow. The same is true of other planets and other professions: Jupiter for politicians; Saturn for scientists; the moon for writers. These professional attributes tend, moreover, to be in line with traditional astrological law which has always associated Mars with competitive spirit, Jupiter with politics, Saturn with concentration, the moon with imagination, and so on.[6]

Refer to Figure 7 (p. 189) for an example of the way this kind of data is presented. The chart shown is basically a graph turned into a circle, so that the larger and larger circles emanating from the centre like ripples on a pool indicate frequency, or number, while the circle itself represents the 360 degrees of the sky. The 'chart' here is therefore a composite of all the birth charts examined in one particular test, superimposed, one over the other onto one 'mean' chart. There are twelve different sectors marked out for examination here, rather like the houses in a normal astrological chart. A solid line is then plotted between each sector showing the number of 'hits' for the particular planet under consideration. Clearly there is a peak around the Ascendant and the MC of the charts examined. The planet in question appears in these sectors far more often, when examining a group of charts, than in the other sectors, and the chances against this are extremely remote unless astrology is, indeed, a reality.

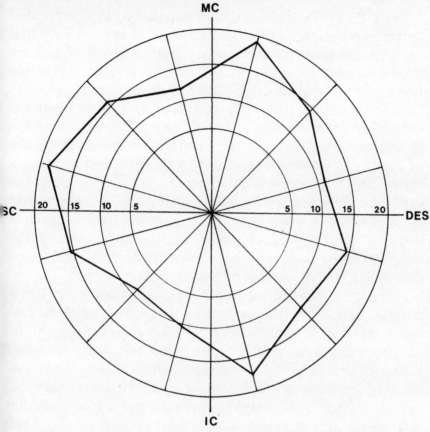

Figure 7.   An example of the way that astrological statistics may be presented (see text)

Gauquelin has also revealed startling relationships between the birth charts of parents and children. If a certain
planet, say Jupiter, is strong in the chart of any one or both
of the parents, then there is an above average chance of it
being so in the chart of the child. But, as we have already
seen, this applies to natural births only. When births are
forced or manipulated the effect disappears.[7] This discovery
of a natural hereditary/planetary link is perhaps one of the
most startling and relevant findings of all. The social significance alone is quite staggering.

Over the years these experiments have been expanded and replicated; the work continues still. However, note that occasionally those hostile to Gauquelin and astrology have replicated the experiments in an incomplete and unfair fashion and produced inconclusive findings. These have usually outraged impartial observers and have been the subject of much scandal and bickering.[8] The most common ploy in these replication experiments is to choose birth data of those not especially eminent in their respective professions: the also-rans of sport, for example. Naturally the astrological correlations of the original research disappear in these cases. The 'eminence effect', as it has been termed, is essential to this kind of research; generally speaking the conclusions of Gauquelin have been reinforced many more times than they have been unjustly refuted.

It must be pointed out, however, that Gauquelin's discovery, or rather confirmation of particular planetary features, is but a minute part of the overall system of astrological usage, most of which still remains unproved; Gauquelin himself remains uncommitted to the overall validity of the subject. Obviously he accepts certain factors — his 'Mars effect' for example — but until proof is on hand for the other tenets of astrology (and there are indeed many yet to be examined) he cautiously reserves judgement, exemplifying the true spirit of scientific and empirical research, which many of his critics would do well to emulate.

ENTER THE NEOFATALISTS

Encouraged by the results obtained by Gauquelin and others, statistics has now become a fashionable subject within the serious astrological community, almost a kind of lifeline for some, promising rewards of approval and acceptance undreamed of since the Enlightenment. Experiments abound, despite warnings from other, perhaps less divinely discontented astrologers that the subject does not lend itself to reductionist study. The warnings emphasise that the business is only intelligible when each of the many separate factors is blended and synthesised into a meaningful whole. However, astrology's champions of research still persist in isolating single discrete factors such as sun signs, or single aspects, or positive/negative polarity, and then setting up statistical programs to relate these to traits such as physical dexterity, genius, propensity to crime, suicide, and so on.

Enthusiasm for such work is fuelled by the statistical axiom that providing you take a large enough sample of subjects, even a weak, isolated factor should eventually show up in the figures — like a tendency for more soldiers to be born when the sun is in the martial sign of Aries, and other simplistic arguments of that nature. Those astrologers who are aware of the reductionist dilemma tend to view this as rather an odd notion however, one which seems to infer that, although two wrongs do not necessarily make a right, several thousand might — just — if you stick at it long enough. Sadly, results when they have occurred have invariably failed to stand up to the most important aspect of statistical doctrine, that of replication. Many of the arguments on which experimentation is based turn out to be both naive and prejudiced, so that seemingly trivial technical points often destroy the basis of the project itself.

This is also the case when attempts are valiantly made to do what are termed whole chart or global studies, which, for example, may feature the examination of anonymous charts which are then related back to their owners through normal procedures of interpretation and synthesis. In other words, can the astrologers match the birth charts to the personalities of their owners without knowing who they are? Carlson's experiment mentioned earlier was a rather sophisticated example of this kind.

191

Here, difficulty frequently arises in establishing an independent measure of the personalities of the volunteers. Again, this was only too evident in the above experiment with the CPIs. So the astrologer is asked to relate the charts to other more concrete features such as profession. Is it possible to locate the chart for the librarian, or the one for the musician? The answer is usually yes, with results far better than chance would normally allow, for example the experiments of Vernon Clark (1961 and 1970), Dobyns (1975 and 1976) and Vidmar (1979).[9]

On a more popular level, there was a recent experiment in which a panel of four astrologers managed to guess correctly eight out of twelve sun signs after a brief interview with each of the dozen subjects. Statistically significant.[10] However, all these experiments have been criticised owing to their basic lack of practical value. An element of clever guesswork or even ESP could have been operative in these cases. As one commentator has already remarked, these experiments do not necessarily demonstrate that astrology works but only that astrologers do.

It is also possible that the rather unsavoury nature of such 'party tricks' could ultimately damage astrology itself, because the natural extension of such an attitude would be experiments in which, say, the astrologers are given a dozen charts of murderers and a dozen of nice guys with instructions to distinguish which charts belong to the murderers and which to the nice guys. The idea that this would be in some way possible is an appalling one which utterly negates the fundamental principle of free will and moral integrity. Does a man have no choice as to whether he must become a murderer or a librarian? And if he does have a choice, why bother to submit his birth chart to statistical analysis in the first place?

Any man or woman is much more than a passive projection of their horoscope at birth. This should be obvious to all, and yet for many the paradox of statistical astrology remains invisible. On the one hand they assert, as do all respectable astrologers, that free will is paramount to the interpretation and workings of any individual chart. Yet on the other they maintain that certain horoscopic factors exert influence detectable by statistics and which experts can spot instantly, as though picking out rotten apples from a barrel. If this is so, then astrologers can safely kiss goodbye to any pretence at being free of fatalistic dogma. The destinies of whole groups of people become subordinate to the trivial little factors that statisticians have supposedly isolated in their charts.

As an enthusiast of astrology, you will need to be aware of this paradox, and the mistake of those who try to turn astrology into a quantifiable science, for by so doing they will also have to turn human nature into one. This is not only an appalling proposition but also an impossible one. Be aware of this temptation, and be aware also of those who might enlist you for experiments already primed to fail, either through naivety or simple deviousness. Remember that you cannot have free will as well as cut-and-dried astrological correlations. Astrologers can't have it both ways. Perhaps it is time we woke up to this fact and returned to interpreting charts for whole people and not just bits of them.

For the moment, however, this is unlikely to happen. Statistical research continues to attract some of the best minds in the profession. Evidence is passionately sought after. There is a burning thirst for scientific respectability, gaining more and more momentum with every new flick of the computer on-switch. The idea seems to be that now statistical proof of a few basic fragments of astrological lore has been demonstrated, it is surely only a matter of time before the scientific establishment sees the potential of the subject, takes it into the hallowed halls of its universities and research labs and begins throwing inordinate sums of money at it. So far, however, things have not quite worked out that way. The scientific community continues to regard the would-be cosmobiologist as a nuisance. The claim that astrology is somehow a poor relative of physics or engineering or biology, and is just waiting to be transformed into a formal white-coated technology is rightly seen as absurd.

These neofatalists of the astrological community who forget that scientists are people too, with pride, fears and anxieties, just like anyone else are not going to do themselves much good by waving statistics in their faces just in order to prove a handful of astrological commonplaces, which are, ultimately, of little practical use. Scientists are not overly pleased when someone borrows the tools of their trade in order, as they see it, to discredit the foundations of their belief and purpose. Nor are astrologers going to exactly endear themselves to the scientists by constantly voicing, in their journals and at their conferences, vague cynical opinions pertaining to the so-called 'crises' in science.

Science, to the extent that most of us perceive it, is hardly in crisis. The method of reasoning, experimentation and projection of rational scientific values into our daily lives continues to be responsible for an almost unbelievable increase in our well-being and happiness, our health and our liberty. And if there are subtle difficulties at the elevated levels of unified field theories or particle physics that challenge traditional materialistic views, it is hardly the place for an astrologer to smugly point them out as if these in some way condone simple irrationality in whatever rough-and-ready, arbitrary form he or she chooses to present it. The ordinary people in the street know nothing of such subtleties. They are, on the whole, rather happy and pleased with what science has done in recent times. For them such complaints can only be mildly redolent of the Inquisition.

Slinging mud at science is not going to make astrology shine. Moreover, criticising the big boys' game while at the same time trying to muscle in on the periphery may actually have been instrumental in whipping up the hostility of the scientific establishment in the first place. It is open to question whether astrology needs to join the game at all. Astrology is already so rich and comprehensive a subject — embracing, as it does, the whole spectrum of mankind's creative, religious, artistic and psychological aspirations — that to waste time and energy paying homage to the scientific establishment seems decidedly superfluous.

Yes, statistics can be impressive, admirable: they really do prove things. But rarely is anyone impressed unless the statistics already back up existing opinions or prejudices. This is as true for the academic specialist as it is for the lay person. Interesting statistics mean little to a scientist who has spent a lifetime using them as a tool of atheism or warfare, nor do they mean much to the person who has spent a whole evening winning, inexplicably, at the roulette wheels, nor to the person who has just been struck by lightning.

So astrologers beware! Ultimately, rather than establish security and acceptance, this continuously unrequited love affair with science could in the future only serve to alienate astrology still further from the vast bulk of the general public who, mistakenly it would seem, once regarded it as a study pertaining to human feelings and desires, rather than to vast bundles of graphs and equations.

Like astrology itself, statistics enable us to impose order onto the vast and magnificent complexity of nature, to unravel the fascinating puzzles that surround us and to help answer some of the terrible questions about being alive. Unlike astrology, however, which rejoices in the mystery and infinite subtlety of our world, statistics place a cold, limiting straight-jacket upon our imaginations, our independent volition and our dignity. In the way of all temporal laws and systems of measurement and analysis, it suffers from the limitations of reductionism: the whole becomes lost in the search for detail. In the years ahead, it would be a shame if, in order to buy a little transient prestige and rank, astrology needed to descend permanently to that level.

CHAPTER 13
FINAL PEP TALK

You have by now at least scanned this book, hopefully with a view to studying it in detail and learning how to defend yourself in practice. Confidence in the form will help with the essential business of improvisation so vital to successful self-defence. Added to this, perhaps the most important ingredient of all, courage or sheer 'bottle', has to be cultivated. Examples are legion of distinguished masters of the martial arts freezing in moments of real attack: on the street, for example, away from the gymnasium or club. Knowing the moves is not enough, you have to have the fluency and the strength of your own convictions to be effective.

At the back of many an astrologer's mind, particularly the less professionally successful or amateur astrologer, may often lie a nagging insecurity or doubt. 'Is it really right? Does it really work? Am I really on the right track or simply deluding myself?' Every astrologer at some stage in his or her career or apprenticeship suffers from such doubts. It can happen to the most experienced as well as to the beginner. Often you will compare your aspirations with a distinct lack of practical or tangible results and wonder if there is any authenticity in astrology at all.

This is not only a sad state but also a rather arrogant one, since it supposes that just because you yourself cannot secure tangible or conclusive results, that the entire body of learning and thought that has constituted astrology over the centuries is somehow worthless. This may be understandable at times of personal crises when self-confidence and self-esteem may vanish for a while, but it is just a little conceited. It is also wrong.

Do not worry, you are certainly not alone. Apart from your own moments of doubt, you will soon discover, from a simple glance through the various journals, books, and papers on the subject, that nowhere is the validity of modern astrology questioned as frequently and exhaustively as among modern astrologers themselves. Current research and experimentation sets an extremely rigorous standard of verification, while traditional tenets are questioned continuously with a critical attitude verging on mistrust and, sometimes, even contempt. Honesty and integrity as well as those occasional bursts of cynicism and self-doubt proliferate to such a degree that indeed astrology often seems to be its own worst enemy. Nothing is taken on face value; nothing is sacred.

Well, who can blame us! For the paradox facing the enthusiast of astrology in modern times is as painful as that facing any other thinking, sensitive individual, be he an artist, a philosopher or theologian: anyone who instinctively adheres to a belief-system based on intangibles, on the feelings, the emotions and the mind. It is the paradox of spirit contending with matter, the cogent world of the senses. In a society where so many values are measured in terms of material evidence and financial reward, it is really only to be expected that this 'inner' experience will be viewed with less importance or even less credibility than the amazing physical presence of, say, your average suspension bridge or microprocessor.

This physical world of machinist miracles has now become the sole testing ground for truth. Can we see it, touch it, feel it? If the answer is no, then it is not real; it is irrelevant. Simple as that. People want and expect results, the surety of the sense-experience before they will listen to your strange ideas. Where is astrology's microchip or video recorder to set the senses tingling! We do not have it. And

197

although astrology is a truly Uranian subject, capable of bridging the rifts between the mental, spiritual and physical worlds, we are not likely to ever deal directly in that particular brand of miracles: the 'hard' miracles of the senses.

Do not be intimidated, however. Do not be put off. For the great objective mechanical view of life contains one encouraging paradox once you start to think and question. Matter itself, the logical catalyst around which all our ideas of modern reality have hitherto evolved, has now been shown, through relativity theory and quantum mechanics, to be actually non-existent, when viewed from its perspective. Mass, gravitation, reality itself, is simply energy — and what energy is no one quite knows. Energy? It's a word, a name, but what's in a name?

Never must you view science as an enemy, therefore. Those at the apex of the scientific pyramid are often sympathetic to the spirit of life and its infinite subtlety. Their research has often led them to touch upon that very quality, while the things that really make the world go round, feelings, ideas, loves and passions, are only comprehensible through the great philosophical and theological systems of humanity, within which astrology has always been celebrated and highly esteemed.

The secret is not to fall into the trap of doubt, of envy for the machinists and their toy miracles. Admittedly, it might not only be your friends, colleagues or relatives but also much of the social establishment and economic world view which will seem to be against you at times. Possibly these will be lifelong adversaries, the hard work and dreams of our statisticians not withstanding. You will simply have to get used to it.

Even in the light of recent experiments, such as the work of Gauquelin or Nelson, and the obvious 'perks' these bring to astrology, the scientific world remains unimpressed, the lay person oblivious. Conventional scholarship has a remarkable talent for absorbing any development such as Nelson's, of taking it under its wing and simply flying away. His work, as with the pioneering discoveries of Piccardi, may well be destined to form yet another thread in astronomy's vast network of force fields, electromagnetic, atomic or otherwise, that generally succeeds in explaining away the miraculous.

The soldier's maxim is divide and conquer: the technologist's is name it and conquer. For how often, except through personification or myth, does the naming of a thing rob it of its wonder and magic, its potency as a moving force within the psyche! The self-styled 'sidereal scientists' have already taken the bait. It is sad. Perhaps they should just bear in mind that our cynical godless era is, so far, brief in comparison to the history of humanity. It is likely that a balance of spirit will return in time. Of course, whether this is to be sooner or later depends a lot on us , on people just like you and me.

Now there's an interesting thought!

If you want it to happen, if you believe in progress, then you will already realise just how important the return of equilibrium between spirit and matter is going to be. When it comes, this new balance will have to treat all of life, all ideas and occupations with equal respect, awarding merely varying degrees of cogency to all the wide and varied affairs of people — a Spectrum of Certainty, if you like, with the solid manifest wonders of engineering and technology, bridges and skyscrapers, microprocessors and video at one end of the scale and the less tangible elements of life: the arts, love, ecstasy, and the metaphysical world of religion and philosophy, towards the other.

This Spectrum of Certainty must admit all aspects of humanity, all facets of being alive, none being superior to the other but each having its place on the scale of physical certainty and regularity. You can predict the results of engineering with almost complete confidence; they are at one end. But the effects of music on the heart comes out with far less certainty. Likewise astrology will fit in somewhere on the spectrum; where exactly must depend on the astrologer himself. It will be, wherever it falls, valid. All things are. Just like the real rainbow spectrum — which is, the physicists tell us, part of a much wider electromagnetic scale which our eyes limit to certain wavelengths only — just like that real rainbow of light, the Spectrum of Certainty will always be limited by our own personal breadth of vision, or that of our race and culture.

Yet it can grow, and that must be where astrology is heading right now: expanding from within. It is really so vast a subject, capable of such breadth that it extends perhaps further off the scale than most of us can imagine. It is worth pursuing, however, and will lead to the pot of gold, the real treasure at the end of the rainbow. What that treasure actually consists of is perhaps different for each of us. Some people call it God. And indeed why shouldn't they!

So go ahead — go get it! Don't be discouraged. There is no need to fear anyone, no need to scrape to anybody else. Astrology is worthy enough in its own right. You can best serve astrology by fighting under your own true colours, and, if a professional in the field, you can best demonstrate its validity by simply working . . . by being of use to the community and, above all, by becoming continually more and more accurate: by simply being right, and in serving those who come to listen.

Astrology is an idea, perhaps the patriarch in the family of great and magnificent ideas that have continually nourished and shaped humanity. Indeed, we are all of us astrologers, and as astrologers we should no more seek to address ourselves to the dull technocrat than to any other specialised representative of society, no more than to the politician or the theologian, the financier or the guru, the industrialist or the child.

Astrology is greater than any one discipline or lifestyle. It is of importance because it touches upon the raw, emotive level of life to which everyone, but everyone, ultimately relates, no matter who or what he or she is, no matter what position he or she holds in society. Astrology is totally relevant, therefore, and you must never doubt its worth. It is a direct link to that pot of gold, the source of all knowledge and experience that progresses and unfolds continually into the future. As it moves, and as you move with it, you will find that it echoes the very metabolism and life-stuff of the human body, and therefore the body of humanity also, mind and soul.

I believe it is the North American Indians who have a saying, 'Walk in pride.' Do so, and you will never need to look back.

NOTES AND REFERENCES

Chapter Six

1. Lao Tzu, *Tao Te Ching*, trans Ch'u Ta-Kao, George Allen & Unwin, 1959.

Chapter Eight

1. Pagan, I., *Signs of the Zodiac Analysed*, original title of *From Pioneer to Poet*, Theosophical Publishing House, 1911.
2. Gauquelin, M., *The Truth About Astrology*, Basil Blackwell, 1983.

Chapter Nine

1. West, J. & Toonder, J., *The Case for Astrology*, Penguin. Contains some interesting photographs of time twins, though some details in the stories have been discredited by later research.
2. Eysenck, H.J. & Nias, D.K.B., *Astrology, Science or Superstition?* Maurice Temple Smith, 1982.
3. West, J. & Toonder, J., *The Case for Astrology*, Penguin.
4. ibid.
5. Dean, G. & Mather, A., *Recent Advances in Natal Astrology*, Analogic, Perth, 1977. Or from The Astrological Association, England.
6. ibid.
7. Gorman, P., *Pythagoras, A Life*, Routledge & Kegan Paul, 1979.
8. Lerner, M., *The Astrological Journal*, XXVIII no. 4. This contains an article describing Lerner's nuclear trigger or axis, and his subsequent predictions of important events related to the atomic industry. In his own periodical, *Welcome to Planet Earth*, Lerner successfully predicted, as early as 1983, a major disaster in the nuclear field between late January and mid-May, 1986. Regarding the capsising of the ship, *The Herald of Free Enterprise*, in 1987, see *The Astrological Journal*, XXIX no. 3: apparently Dennis Elwell sent a registered letter to the owners of the ship warning of potential danger just days before the tragedy.

9. *The Prophecies of Nostradamus*, Neville Spearman, 1973.

10. *The Astrological Journal*, XXIV no. 4. Swiss Journal, *Cosmotrend*, for Angermeyer.

11. Gleadow, R., *The Origins of the Zodiac*, Jonathan Cape, 1968. And Walters, D., *Chinese Astrology*, Aquarian Press, 1987.

12. Lindsay, J., *Origins of Astrology*, Frederick Muller, 1971.

13. Neugebauer, O., *The Exact Sciences in Antiquity*, Brown University Press, 1957. Contains many interesting illustrations, monuments, tombs, etc., from ancient times.

14. Yates, F., *The Art of Memory*, Routledge & Kegan Paul, 1966.

15. Webb, E., *The Names of the Stars*, Nisbet & Co., London, 1952.

16. Manilius, *Astronomica*, Loeb Edition, Heinemann, London, 1977.

17. Gauquelin, M., *How Cosmic and Atmospheric Energies Influence Your Health*, Aurora Press, New York, 1971.

18. Jung, C., commentary included in *The Secret of the Golden Flower*, the Chinese Classic translated by Richard Wilhelm. Routledge & Kegan Paul, 1962.

19. Gauquelin, M., *The Truth About Astrology*, Basil Blackwell, 1983.

20. Hoyle, F., *The Intelligent Universe*, Michael Joseph, 1983.

21. ibid.

22. Tillyard, E., *The Elizabethan World Picture*, Chatto & Windus, 1945.

23. Aquinas, St Thomas, *Summa Theologica*.

24. Gauquelin, M., *The Truth about Astrology*, Basil Blackwell, 1983.

25. ibid.

26. ibid.

27. Robbins, R., *An Encyclopedia of Witchcraft and Demonology*, Spring Books, London, 1964.

28. Gettings, F., *The Hidden Art*, Cassell, 1978.

29. For a clear, objective discussion on the origins of Christianity see: Russell, B., *History of Western Philosophy*, George Allen & Unwin, 1946.

30. Hall, J., *A History of Ideas and Images in Italian Art*, John Murry, 1983.

31. Gettings, F., *The Hidden Art*, Cassell, 1978.

32. Hall, J., *A History of Ideas and Images in Italian Art*, John Murry, 1983.

33. Jung, C., His memorial address to Richard Wilhelm, contained in *The Secret of the Golden Flower*, Routledge & Kegan Paul, 1931.

34. Watson, L., *Supernature*, Hodder & Stoughton, 1973. And for a typically severe critique of Nelson's system, see Eysenck, H. & Nias, D., *Astrology, Science or Superstition?* Maurice Temple Smith, 1982.

35. ibid.

36. Watson, L., *Supernature*, Hodder & Stoughton, 1973.

37. Eysenck, H. & Nias, D., *Astrology, Science or Superstition?* Maurice Temple Smith, 1982.

38. McGillion, F., *The Opening Eye*, Coventure Ltd., London, 1980.
39. ibid.
40. ibid.
41. Dean, G. and others, *Recent Advances in Natal Astrology*, Analogic, Perth, 1977.
42. Eysenck, H. & Nias, D., *Astrology, Science or Superstition?* Maurice Temple Smith, 1982. And Watson, L., *Supernature*, Hodder & Stoughton, 1973.
43. ibid.
44. ibid.
45. Gauquelin, M., *How Cosmic and Atmospheric Energies Influence Your Health*, Aurora Press, New York, 1971.
46. Eysenck, H. & Nias, D., *Astrology, Science or Superstition?* Maurice Temple Smith, 1982. And Watson, L., *Supernature*, Hodder & Stoughton, 1973. And see too Gauquelin, M., *How Cosmic and Atmospheric Energies Influence Your Health*, Aurora Press, New York, 1971.
47. ibid.
48. ibid.
49. Kollerstrom, N., *Astrochemistry, a Study of Metal-Planet Affinities*, Emergence Press, 1984. And various papers in *The Astrological Journal*, XVIX no. 3, with Drummond, M. & Kollerstrom, N., XXIV no. 4.
50. ibid. And also Pelikan, W., *The Secrets of Metals*, Anthroposophical Press, 1973, trans from the original German.
51. Capra, F., *The Tao of Physics*, Bantam, 1977. See also Barrow, J. & Tipler, F., *The Anthropic Cosmological Principle*, Oxford University Press, 1986.
52. Gauquelin, M., numerous original papers but summed up readily for the general reader, with references of course, in his book, *The Truth about Astrology*, Basil Blackwell, 1983.
53. ibid.
54. Addey, J., *Harmonics in Astrology*, L.N. Fowler, 1976. And editions of the *Astrological Journal* for 1967.
55. Gauquelin, M., *How Cosmic and Atmospheric Energies Influence Your Health*, Aurora Press, New York, 1971.
56. Piccardi, G., *The Chemical Basis of Medical Climatology*, Thomas Books, Illinois, 1963. Or summed up easily in Gauquelin, M., *How Cosmic and Atmospheric Energies Influence Your Health*, Aurora Press, New York, 1971.
57. Jung, C., *Synchronicity: An Acausal Connecting Principle*, Routledge & Kegan Paul, 1955.
58. Barrow, J. & Tipler, F., *The Anthropic Cosmological Principle*, Oxford University Press, 1986.
59. See any of the excellent volumes by the psychotherapist Liz Green, currently (1990) Patron of the Faculty of Astrological Studies. Books include *Relating, Saturn, The Astrology of Fate*, from Aquarian Press and others.

60. For those interested in this field, current research is now being coordinated by the Urania Trust and the Astrological Association. See list of useful addresses, p. 215.

61. Palant, D., *The Astrological Journal*, XXV no. 2, and the Editorial of XXIX no. 4.

62. Watters, B., *Horary Astrology and the Judgement of Events*, Valhalla, 1973. And for one of the best examples of all, see Barclay, O., *The Astrological Journal*, XXV no. 4, letters section, and the celebrated story of Max, the lost cat.

Chapter Ten

1. Kollerstrom, N., *Astrochemistry. A Study of Metal-Planet Affinities*, Emergence Press, 1984.

Chapter Eleven

1. Lao Tzu, *Tao Te Ching*, trans. Chu' Ta-Kao. George Allen & Unwin, 1959.

2. Obviously translations vary. Conventional biographers, however, are pretty consistent in their unwillingness to transmit Kepler's real views on the subject. Standard biographical works include: Caspar, M., *Kepler*, trans. Hellman, C.D., Abelard-Schumann, 1959. And Koestler, A., *Watershed: A Biography of Johannes Kepler*, Doubleday, 1960. See also Graubard, M., *Astrology's Decline and Its Bearing On the Decline and Death of Beliefs*, Osiris, 1958. And even the BBC's otherwise excellent Open University production on Kepler and his ideas.

3. Lao Tzu, *Tao Te Ching*, trans. Gia-Fu Feng & English, J., Wildwood House, 1973.

Chapter Twelve

1. 'Objections to Astrology', a statement by 186 leading scientists, *Humanist* 35, no. 5. Sept/Oct 1975.

2. The journal, *Aquarian Agent*, 1976.

3. Mayo, J., White, O., Eysenck, H., *The Journal of Social Psychology*, 1978. Eysenck, H. & Nias, D., *Astrology, Science or Superstition?* Maurice Temple Smith, 1982. And see also Jeff Mayo's defence of his later work and replications in *The Astrological Journal*, XXVIII nos. 4 and 5.

4. Carlson, S., *A Double-Blind Test of Astrology*, Nature vol. 318, no. 6045, 1985.

5. *The Astrological Journal*, April, 1986, describing a communication from T.W. Hamilton.

6. Gauquelin, M., *The Truth About Astrology*, Basil Blackwell, 1983. And abridged English translations of the original papers now available in Gauquelin's *Written in the Stars*, Aquarian, 1988.

7. Gauquelin, M., *The Truth About Astrology*, Basil Blackwell, 1983.

8. ibid.

9. Dean, G. and others, *Recent Advances in Natal Astrology: A Critical Review 1900–1976*, Analogic, Perth, 1977. (Distributed by Recent Advances, c/o The Astrological Association. See Useful Addresses, p. 215.)

10. ibid.

GLOSSARY OF TERMS

Ascendant This usually refers to the degree of the zodiac sign which is rising in the birth chart. In popular conversation, however, it can refer to the whole sign. It is of at least equal importance to the sun sign when judging character.

Aspects Angular relationships within the chart that draw together the characters of the planets in certain ways. There are several aspects, each corresponding to an exact division of the circle. However, an allowance, or 'orb', of several degrees either side of exactitude is permitted, and it is the narrowness or otherwise of this orb which indicates the strength of the aspect itself.

Astrology The ancient art of determining character and forecasting trends through judgement of celestial events.

Astronomy The scientific measurement of celestial phenomena. Speculation on the size, shape, age, etc., of the universe. Prior to the Renaissance, a term synonymous with astrology.

Celestial Equator The earth's equator projected onto the sphere of the heavens. A great circle, therefore, at 90 degrees to the earth's axis of rotation.

Chart   An accurate map of the sky for the exact time and place of an event — usually a birth. The chart forms the basis of all serious astrological work.

Constellations   Ancient star patterns still used by scientists as a means of nomenclature. Although a constellation, say Pisces, can share the same name as the astrologer's sign 'Pisces', it has little to do with it except in historical terms.

Cusp   Means 'border-line'. People 'born on the cusp' are those whose birthdays occur when the sun is changing signs. A cusp in astrology also means the dividing line between houses as well as signs.

Equinoctial Points   Two places in the sky where the celestial equator cuts the ecliptic. The sun positioned on these points indicates equal length of day and night anywhere on earth, and the spring equinoctial point for the northern hemisphere always indicates the starting point of the zodiac, and consequently of the first sign, Aries.

Ecliptic   A great circle in the sky traced by the apparent motion of the sun as the earth orbits about it once every 365 days. The ecliptic is the centre-line of the zodiac, which ranges around eight degrees above and below it. The ecliptic is inclined to the earth's equator at an angle of around 23 degrees, and it is this phenomenon that produces the cycle of the seasons.

Elements   Each sign has its element, or mode of expression; planets vary slightly in character according to the element in which each is found. In Western astrology we work with four elements: Fire, Earth, Air and Water.

Geocentric   Earth-centred or in orbit about the earth.

Heliocentric   Sun-centred or in orbit about the sun.

Horary (Latin 'of the hour'.) The branch of astrology dealing with specific questions and the judgement of events.

Houses Segments of the chart, twelve in number, and commencing at the Ascendant. Each house pertains to certain fields of activity, to certain people or places. For instance, the seventh house relates, among other things, to partners and rivals; the tenth house to career and parental influences. There is nothing in the world that is not covered by one of the twelve houses of astrology.

MC Abbreviation for the latin *Medium Coeli*, or the point where the ecliptic crosses the local meridian. Due south on the zodiac, in other words.

Meridian Usually refers to the local meridian, or great circle that passes through the zenith (overhead) and the north and south points of the horizon.

Midpoint A point between two bodies in the chart. There are many of these, of course, but they are only relevant when a third body is contacted, either by conjunction or by aspect to that point. Midpoints can provide much additional detail in natal work and any worthwhile analysis should always at least consider them along with the more basic features of the chart.

Mundane Astrology Political astrology. Nations and peoples. Economics.

Polarity There are six positive and six negative signs in the zodiac, the terms being roughly synonymous with extraversion or introversion respectively, or the Yang and Yin of Chinese philosophy. The characters of planets can vary slightly according to the polarity of the sign in which each is found.

Planet Technically a planet is any large body in orbit about a star, including our own sun which is also a star, only very close. In astrology, however, both the moon and the sun are termed 'planets'. The positions of such bodies are constantly changing in relation to the earth, and it is this, along with the rotation of the earth itself, that creates the many variables of astrology, moment to moment, chart to chart. The glyphs for the planets are as follows:

SUN ☉ MOON ☽ MERCURY ☿ VENUS ♀

MARS ♂ JUPITER ♃ SATURN ♄ URANUS ♅

NEPTUNE ♆ PLUTO ♇

Precession More fully: precession of the equinoxes. Due to a slight 'wobble' of the earth's axis, rather like the wobble of a spinning top, the ecliptic circle moves around the celestial equator once every 22 000 years or so, taking the equinoctial points, and thus the zodiac itself, along with it. The zodiac is therefore seen to vary in relation to the background of fixed stars, or constellations as they are called. Around 2000 years ago, the signs and the constellations shared the same names and roughly the same places in the sky. Now, however, the zodiac signs have moved on, and the sign Aries has drifted into the section of the sky occupied by the stars of the ancient constellation of Pisces. This creates considerable confusion for the lay person. Astronomers and map makers, though, being perhaps more traditionally oriented than astrologers, have since the time of Ptolemy (2nd century AD) refused to change the constellation boundaries to keep pace with precession.

Progressions Term used for the most popular method of forecasting. Positions in the progressed chart for any period are compared to natal positions to determine trends and developments.

212

Ruler Each sign, and also each house has what is called a 'ruler'. For example, the planet Mercury always rules the signs Gemini and Virgo. It can also rule one or more houses in the individual chart. This house rulership is determined by the location of the house cusp. If, say, your 7th house cusp falls in the sign Virgo (ruled by Mercury) then we know that the movements and relative strengths of Mercury will relate closely to all 7th house matters: in other words partners or rivals.

Transit In astrology this usually means any situation where a planet's current position creates a cross-aspect to a feature in a birth chart.

Zodiac A narrow band in the sky extending around eight degrees either side of the ecliptic, or annual path traced by the sun. It is divided into twelve equal sections, or signs — echoing the hexagonal pattern found so often in nature, the snow-flake, for example. The glyphs for the signs are written as follows:

ARIES ♈   TAURUS ♉   GEMINI ♊   CANCER ♋

LEO ♌   VIRGO ♍   LIBRA ♎   SCORPIO ♏

SAGITTARIUS ♐   AQUARIUS ♒

CAPRICORN ♑   PISCES ♓

USEFUL ADDRESSES

If you wish to contact a good astrologer in your area, a school or a local group, but do not have a personal recommendation, then it may be possible to do so by writing to one of the sources in the following list. However, note that many of these organisations do not have headquarters as such. They are often run by volunteers, and are usually non-profit making. So do please enclose a large stamped addressed envelope with any enquiry.

The Company of Astrologers, 6 Queen Square, Bloomsbury, London WClN 3AR.

Faculty of Astrological Studies, BM 7470, London WC1N 3XX (Faculty instructors are resident in the UK and USA).

Astrological Association of Great Britain, 4 Rough Heys Lane, Marton, Blackpool FY4 5AG.

The Mayo School of Astrology, Alvana Gardens, Tregavethan, Truro, Cornwall TR4 9EN.

Qualifying Horary Correspondence Course, Mongeham Lodge Cottage, Great Mongeham, Kent CT14 OHD.

The Urania Trust, ASC, 396 Caledonian Road, London N1 1DN.

The Centre for Psychological Astrology, PO Box 890, London NW5 2NE.

The Advisory Panel on Astrological Education, 163 Hever Avenue, West Kingsdown, Sevenoaks, Kent

The Astrological Lodge of London, BM Astrolodge, London WC1N 3XX.

American Federation of Astrologers, PO Box 22040, Tempe, AZ85282, USA.

Aquarius Workshops Inc., PO Box 556, Encino, CA91426, USA.

National Centre for Geocosmic Research, 850 Success Avenue, Lakeland, Florida 33801, USA.

SUGGESTED READING LIST

CAPRA, F., *The Tao of Physics*, Bantam, 1977. An eminent scientist discussing the similarities between particle physics and mysticism.

CARTER, C., *The Principles of Astrology*, Theosophical Publishing House Ltd., 1925. An old book but still one of the best introductions to the subject available.

GALANTE, L., *Tai Chi, The Supreme Ultimate*, Samuel Weiser, USA, 1982. Good exposition on the Chinese art of Tai Chi Chuan and how it can relate to the modern world.

GAUQUELIN, M., *The Truth About Astrology*, Basil Blackwell, 1983. A good, all-round summary for the general reader of the work of this remarkable man.

GAUQUELIN, M., *How Cosmic and Atmospheric Energies Influence Your Health*, Aurora Press, New York, 1981. Meteorology and astronomy combine here to make fascinating reading.

GETTINGS, F., *The Hidden Art*, Cassell, 1978. The first few chapters dealing with the esoteric dimension of Christian art are superb.

HALL, J., *A History of Ideas and Images in Italian Art*, John Murray, 1983. Interesting to learn the degree to which astrological and mystical images exist in the Church.

HALL, M.P., *The Secret Teachings of All Ages*, The Philosophical Research Society, USA. Available in UK through Aquarian Press. A wonderfully illustrated and comprehensive guide to the mystical dimension of world religions and occult teachings.

HOYLE, F., *The Intelligent Universe*, Michael Joseph, London, 1983. Hoyle, one of the world's leading astrophysicists, explains his research into genetics and the dramatic conclusions that seriously question the Darwinian view of life on earth.

LAO TZU, *Tao Te Ching*, trans. Ch'u Ta-Kao, George Allen & Unwin, 1959. The great Chinese classic of wisdom and Taoist philosophy. There are many translations but this seems as good, if not better, than most.

MAYO, J., *Teach Yourself Astrology*, from the Teach Yourself Series, Pitman, London. Good general introduction.

MAYO, J., *The Astrologer's Astronomical Handbook*, Fowler, 1979. Technical background. An absolute must for all astrologers.

McGILLION, F., *The Opening Eye*, Coventure, London, 1980. Discussion of the pineal gland and its sensitivity to cosmic phenomena.

PAPON, D., *The Lure of the Heavens: A History of Astrology*, Samuel Weiser, New York, 1980. Highly readable history book.

PARKER, D & J., *The New Complete Astrologer*, Mitchell Beazley. Lavish and comprehensive exposition of astrology, its uses and applications in modern affairs.

STASSINOPOULOS, A. & BENY, R., *The Gods of Greece*, Weidenfeld & Nicolson, London, 1983. A beautiful and stimulating account of the Greek gods and their importance as archetypes of the unconscious and, therefore, of astrology.

WATSON, L., *Supernature*, Hodder & Stoughton, 1979. A magical tour of all the various strands of research into astrology and biochemistry, etc. Much hard evidence for the 'life field' and its receptivity to cosmic influences.

YATES, F., *The Art of Memory*, Routledge & Kegan Paul, 1966. Heavy going, but interesting account of the extent to which mnemonics were employed in times gone by.

And for the more specialist reader:

DEAN, G. & MATHER, A., *Recent Advances in Natal Astrology*, Analogic, Perth, 1977. Also available from The Astrological Association of Great Britain. A critical review of just about every piece of serious astrological research and experimentation undertaken this century. Also, an adequate review of the traditional basis of astrological lore. Many of the experiments mentioned in our sections on sparring and combat — the work of Nelson, Piccardi, Gauquelin, Addey and so on — are all summarised skillfully and concisely by Dean and his team. New material is constantly under review, and the interested reader should inquire for further information from the Astrological Association.

EYSENCK, H. & NIAS D., *Astrology, Science or Superstition?* Extremely thorough and well researched book by two eminent statisticians. Eysenck, like Dean, tends to give the benefit of the doubt to the sceptics rather than the astrologer but otherwise this book brings welcome clarity to what is often a notoriously woolly subject.

INDEX

If you have enjoyed reading this book, other titles in the Quantum list will be of interest. These include:

The Dream Lover, Transforming relationships through dreams,
by Les Peto

Dowsing For Health, The applications and methods for holistic healing
by Arthur Bailey

Life Cycles, The astrology of inner space and its application to the rhythms of life
by Bill Anderton

Psychic Sense, Training and developing psychic sensitivity
by Mary Swainson and Louisa Bennett

The Survival Papers, Applied Jungian psychology
by Daryl Sharp

Applied Visualisation, A mind–body programme
by James Lynn Page

Seeds of Magick, An exposé of modern magickal practices
by Catherine Summers and Julian Vayne

The Healing Hand Book, Discover and develop your healing power
by Patrick Butler

Ask your bookseller for full details on the complete range of Quantum titles, or write to the publisher, W. Foulsham & Co. Ltd., Yeovil Road, Slough, Berks. SL1 4JH.